D0875561

MISSING OUT

Also by Adam Phillips

Winnicott
On Kissing, Tickling, and Being Bored
On Flirtation
Terrors and Experts
Monogamy
The Beast in the Nursery
Darwin's Worms
Promises, Promises
Houdini's Box
Equals
Going Sane
Intimacies (with Leo Bersani)
Side Effects
On Kindness (with Barbara Taylor)
The Concise Dictionary of Dress (with Judith Clark)
On Balance

EDITOR OF

Charles Lamb, *Selected Prose*
Walter Pater, *The Renaissance*
Edmund Burke, *A Philosophical Enquiry*
Michael Eigen, *The Electrified Tightrope*
Richard Howard, *Selected Poems* (with Hugh Haughton)
John Clare in Context (with Hugh Haughton
and Geoffrey Summerfield)
The Book of Interruptions (with David Hillman)
General Editor of the new Penguin Modern Classics
Freud translations

MISSING OUT

In Praise of the
Unlived Life

ADAM PHILLIPS

FARRAR, STRAUS AND GIROUX
NEW YORK

Farrar, Straus and Giroux
18 West 18th Street, New York 10011

Copyright © 2012 by Adam Phillips
Printed in the United States of America
Originally published in 2012 by Hamish Hamilton, Great Britain
Published in the United States by Farrar, Straus and Giroux
First American edition, 2013

Owing to limitations of space, all acknowledgements for permission to reprint
previously published material can be found on page 203.

Library of Congress Cataloging-in-Publication Data
Phillips, Adam, 1954–
    Missing out : in praise of the unlived life / Adam Phillips. — 1st ed.
        p.   cm.
    ISBN 978-0-374-28111-3 (alk. paper)
    1. Self-perception.   2. Self-actualization (Psychology)   I. Title.

BF697.5.S43 P485 2012
155.2—dc23

                                                                    2012021524

www.fsgbooks.com
www.twitter.com/fsgbooks • www.facebook.com/fsgbooks

3   5   7   9   10   8   6   4

For Simon Prosser

Omissions are not accidents.

Marianne Moore, epigraph to
The Complete Poems of Marianne Moore

History is not merely what happened; it is what happened in the context of what might have happened.

Hugh Trevor-Roper,
'History and Imagination'

Nobody I know would take advice from Hamlet.

Jennifer Grotz, 'The Nunnery'

Contents

Prologue

The unexamined life is surely worth living, but is the unlived life worth examining? It seems a strange question until one realizes how much of our so-called mental life is about the lives we are not living, the lives we are missing out on, the lives we could be leading but for some reason are not. What we fantasize about, what we long for, are the experiences, the things and the people that are absent. It is the absence of what we need that makes us think, that makes us cross and sad. We have to be aware of what is missing in our lives – even if this often obscures both what we already have and what is actually available – because we can survive only if our appetites more or less work for us. Indeed, we have to survive our appetites by making people cooperate with our wanting. We pressurize the world to be there for our benefit. And yet we quickly notice as children – it is, perhaps, the first thing we do notice – that our needs, like our wishes, are always potentially unmet. Because we are always shadowed by the possibility of not getting what we want, we learn, at best, to ironize our wishes – that is, to call our wants wishes: a wish is only a wish until, as we say, it comes true – and, at worst, to hate our needs. But we also learn to live somewhere between the lives we have and the lives we would like. This book is about some versions of these double lives we can't help but live.

There is always what will turn out to be the life we led, and the life that accompanied it, the parallel life (or lives) that never actually happened, that we lived in our minds, the wished-for life (or lives): the risks untaken and the opportunities avoided or unprovided. We refer to them as our unlived lives because somewhere we believe that they were open to us; but for some reason – and we might spend a great deal of our lived lives trying to find and give the reason – they were not possible. And what was not possible all too easily becomes the story of our lives. Indeed, our lived lives might become a protracted mourning for, or an endless tantrum about, the lives we were unable to live. But the exemptions we suffer, whether forced or chosen, make us who we are. As we know more now than ever before about the kinds of lives it is possible to live – and affluence has allowed more people than ever before to think of their lives in terms of choices and options – we are always haunted by the myth of our potential, of what we might have it in ourselves to be or do. So when we are not thinking, like the character in Randall Jarrell's poem, that 'The ways we miss our lives is life', we are grieving or regretting or resenting our failure to be ourselves as we imagine we could be. We share our lives with the people we have failed to be.

We discover these unlived lives most obviously in our

envy of other people, and in the conscious (and unconscious) demands we make on our children to become something that was beyond us. And, of course, in our daily frustrations. Our lives become an elegy to needs unmet and desires sacrificed, to possibilities refused, to roads not taken. The myth of our potential can make of our lives a perpetual falling-short, a continual and continuing loss, a sustained and sometimes sustaining rage; though at its best it lures us into the future, but without letting us wonder why such lures are required (we become promising through the promises made to us). The myth of potential makes mourning and complaining feel like the realest things we ever do; and makes of our frustration a secret life of grudges. Even if we set aside the inevitable questions – How would we know if we had realized our potential? Where did we get our picture of this potential from? If we don't have potential what do we have? – we can't imagine our lives without the unlived lives they contain. We have an abiding sense, however obscure and obscured, that the lives we do lead are informed by the lives that escape us. That our lives are defined by loss, but loss of what might have been; loss, that is, of things never experienced. Once the next life – the better life, the fuller life – has to be in this one, we have a considerable task on our hands. Now someone is asking us not only to survive but to flourish, not simply or solely to be good but to make the most of our lives. It is a quite different kind of demand. The story of our lives becomes the story of the lives we were prevented from living.

Darwin showed us that everything in life is vulnerable, ephemeral and without design or God-given purpose. For disillusioned non-believers – who, of course, pre-dated Darwin and created the conditions for his work and its reception – belief in God (and providential design) was replaced by belief in the infinite untapped talents and ambitions of human beings (and in the limitless resources of the earth). It became the enduring project of our modern cultures of redemption – cultures committed above all to science and progress – to create societies in which people can realize their potential, in which 'growth' and 'productivity' and 'opportunity' are the watchwords (it is essential to the myth of potential that scarcity is scarcely mentioned: and growth is always possible and expected). And yet, as William Empson wrote in the appropriately entitled *Some Versions of Pastoral*, 'it is only in degree that any improvement of society could prevent wastage of human powers; the waste even in a fortunate life, the isolation even of a life rich in intimacy, cannot but be felt deeply, and is the central feeling of tragedy'. Our wished-for lives, the lives we miss out on, are at once both an acknowledgement of, and part of our toolkit for dealing with, this unavoidable waste. They are the ways – as are the tragedies discussed in this book – of thinking about, of transforming, the isolation and the waste.

Because we are nothing special – on a par with ants and daffodils – it is the work of culture to make us feel special; just as parents need to make their children feel special to help them bear and bear with – and hopefully enjoy – their insignificance in the larger scheme of things. In this sense growing up is always an undoing of what needed to be done: first, ideally, we are made to feel special; then we are expected to enjoy a world in which we are not. After Darwin we have to work out what, other than specialness, might make our lives worth living; after Darwin we can say, when people realize how accidental they are, they are tempted to think of themselves as chosen. We certainly tend to be more special, if only to ourselves, in our (imaginary) unlived lives.

So it is worth wondering what the need to be special prevents us seeing about ourselves – other, that is, than the unfailing transience of our lives; what the need to be special stops us from being. This, essentially, is the question psychoanalysis was invented to address: what kind of pleasures can sustain a creature that is nothing special? Once the promise of immortality, of being chosen, was displaced by the promise of more life – the promise, as we say, of getting more out of life – the unlived life became a haunting presence in a life legitimated by nothing more than the desire to live it. For modern people, stalked by their choices, the good life is a life lived to the full. We become obsessed, in a new way, by what is missing in our lives; and by what sabotages the pleasures that we seek. Childhood is a problem because of the effect it has on the adults we are able to become. No one has ever had the adolescence they should have had. No one has ever taken enough of their chances, or had enough chances to take, and so on.

What is absent and felt to be essential is not, of course, a modern or a secular preoccupation; wanting is what we do to survive, and we want only what isn't there (and it is, indeed, the challenges to our wanting by other people, the clash of our desires with the desires of others, that make us who we are). But psychoanalysis, like Darwinism, was part of a new conversation about how to describe what was missing in our modern lives. Where Darwin wanted to talk of survival as adaptation – thereby rendering everything we call culture simply a toolkit for survival, for getting through life – Freud wanted to talk of survival as pleasure-seeking, and of pleasure-seeking and the avoidance of pain as the only purpose of a life. In the pleasure-seeking picture a life without sufficient pleasure is not worth surviving for (or reproducing). Freud, in other words, like Camus after him – implicitly, but without quite saying so – believed that the only question, if not the only philosophical question, was whether or not to commit suicide. Or, as he suggested: 'the aim of the organism is to die in its own way'. For Freud, the questions for the modern person are not just 'How can I survive?' but 'What makes my life worth living for?' 'What are the pleasures without which I cannot live?' It is among the contentions of this book that our unlived lives – the lives we live in fantasy, the wished-for lives – are often more important to us than our so-called lived lives, and that we can't (in both senses) imagine ourselves without them; that they are an essential part of the ways in which we answer Freud's questions. And it is not incidental to this that in our unlived lives we are rather more transgressive than we tend to be in our lived lives.

We make our lives pleasurable, and therefore bearable, by picturing them as they might be; it is less obvious, though, what these compelling fantasy lives – lives of, as it were, a more complete satisfaction – are a self-cure for. Our solutions tell us what our problems are; our fantasy lives are not – or not necessarily – alternatives to, or refuges from, those real lives but an essential part of them. As some critics of psychoanalysis rightly point out, a lot depends on whether our daydreams – our personal preoccupations – turn into political action (and, indeed, on whether our preferred worlds are shared worlds, and on what kind of sharing goes on in them). There is nothing more obscure than the relationship between the lived and the unlived life. (Each member of a couple, for example, is always having a relationship, wittingly or unwittingly, with their partner's unlived lives; their initial and initiating relationship is between what they assume are their potential selves.) So we may need to think of ourselves as always living a double life, the one that we wish for and the one that we practise; the one that never happens and the one that keeps happening.

'If I wish to limit myself to facts,' Camus writes in *The Myth of Sisyphus*, 'I know what man wants, I know what the world offers him, and now I can say that I also know what links them. I have no need to dig deeper.' This misfit, that is the only fit there is between 'man' and his world, between what he wants and what is on offer, is what Camus calls, a little distractingly, the 'Absurd'. There is a gap between what we want and what we can have, and that gap, Camus says, is our link, our connection, to the world (the absurdity, we might say, is our assumption that the world was made for us; even if our parents more or less suited us, the world probably won't). We can't actually get round our wanting, nor can we get round what is really available; these are what Camus calls the facts (and Freud calls the 'reality principle'). And this discord, this supposed mismatch, is the origin of our experience of missing out, and the origin of engaged political action; as though we believe there is a world elsewhere of what Freud calls 'complete satisfaction', and that Camus might call a more just world. Any ideal, any preferred world, is a way of asking, what kind of world are we living in that makes this the solution (our utopias tell us more about our lived lives, and their privations, than about our wished-for lives); or, to put it more clinically, what would the symptom have to be for this to be the self-cure? In our unlived lives we are always more satisfied, far less frustrated versions of ourselves. In our wishes – which Freud put at the centre of our lives – we bridge the gap between what we are and what we want to be as if by magic; and, by the same token, we sow the seeds of our unlived lives.

In Freud's story our possibilities for satisfaction depend upon our capacity for frustration; if we can't let ourselves feel our frustration – and, surprisingly, this is a surprisingly difficult thing to do – we can't get a sense of what it is we might be wanting, and missing, of what might really give us pleasure (greed is despair about pleasure). Describing how our wanting works, and works against us – how all our wanting has a history – Freud shows us that frustration is at once both the source of our pleasure and the inspiration for our unlived lives. That frustration is where we start from; the child's dawning awareness of himself is an awareness of something necessary not being there. The child becomes present to himself in the absence of something he needs. The experiences described in this book of not getting it, of getting away with it, and of getting out of it are all chapters in our unlived lives, potentially productive forms of ordinary frustration. Missing out on one experience we have another one. And then the comparisons are made. We choose by exclusion. The right choice is the one that makes us lose interest in the alternatives; but we can never know beforehand which the right choice will be. We never know if one frustration will lead to another.

'In general it is also certainly true to say,' Freud wrote in 'Contributions to the Psychology of Erotic Life', 'that the psychical significance of a drive rises in proportion to its frustration.' The more we frustrate ourselves in wanting something, the more we value our desire for it. But Freud is also saying that it is only in states of frustration that we can begin to imagine – to elaborate, to envision – our desire. Though Freud is telling us something here about the plea-sures of asceticism, this is not a counsel of renunciation; he is recommending frustration as the essential preparation for desire, as the precondition for its flourishing, and for the possibility of there being some satisfaction. When we are frustrated, the unlived life is always beckoning; the unlived life of gratified desire returns as a possibility. Waiting too long poisons desire, but waiting too little pre-empts it; the imagining is in the waiting. In con-sciously contrived instant gratification, neither desire nor the object of desire is sufficiently imagined. Wanting takes time; partly because it takes some time to get over the resistances to wanting, and partly because we are often unconscious of what it is that we do want. But the worst thing we can be frustrated of is frustration itself; to be deprived of frustration is to be deprived of the possibili-ties of satisfaction. If we are not, say, to use sex to get rid of sex, if we are not to abolish our pleasure by the too slick seeking of it, we will need to recover, or even to refine, our frustration. We will have to resist our wanting being stolen from us before we have realized it. So before our satisfaction, it is our frustration we need to turn to.

On Frustration

Nothing I know matters more
Than what never happened.

John Burnside, 'Hearsay'

Tragedies are stories about people not getting what they want, but not all stories about people not getting what they want seem tragic. In comedies people get something of what they want, but in tragedies people often discover that their wanting doesn't work, and as the story unfolds they get less and less of what they thought they wanted. Indeed, both what they want and how they go about wanting it wreaks havoc and ultimately destroys the so-called tragic hero and, of course, his enemies and accomplices. Whether it is called ambition, the quest for love, or the search for truth, tragedies expose, to put it as simply as possible, what the unhappy ending of wanting something looks like – of wanting to displace a king, of wanting vengeance for one's father, of wanting a special daughter's love announced. Tragic heroes are failed pragmatists. Their ends are unrealistic and their means are impractical.

Given that we live in a state of permanent need; are,

as the psychoanalyst John Rickman said, 'instinct-ridden', always found wanting, what is it that makes desiring tragic, dire rather than amusing, full of dread rather than full of life? Isaiah Berlin, in a famous pronouncement in 'Two Concepts of Liberty', offered the liberal position: 'If, as I believe, the ends of men are many, and not all of them are in principle compatible with each other, then the possibility of conflict – and of tragedy – can never wholly be eliminated from human life, either personal or social.' We always have competing wants, they are often incompatible, so in making choices essentials are sacrificed. Lives are tragic not merely when people can't have everything they want but when their wanting mutilates them; when what they want entails an unbearable loss. What can be described as tragic about the Oedipus complex, named after a tragedy, is that the child, in the Freudian account, in desiring one parent turns the other into a rival, and ultimately has to relinquish his need for his parents in order to be a wholeheartedly desiring adult. You have to give up being a child, for sex; and that, of course, may not be all you have to give up. The quest, one might say, is the finding out whether it is worth it (it is a variant of 'you must lose your life in order to find it'). Because, in Berlin's terms, our ends are many, and often enough incompatible, devastating losses are some-times entailed. Shakespeare's King Lear wants to divide his kingdom into three, but he wants one third, Cordelia's, to be more 'opulent' than the other two; he wants to relinquish his crown but sustain something of his power; he wants his daughters and sons-in-law to collaborate with him in being his accomplices; he wants to live as he wants, in other people's houses. He loses everything he wants, and everything he needs.

The pragmatist would say that the art of life is in rendering incompatible wants compatible; redescribing them such that they are no longer mutually exclusive (Lear might say to Cordelia, 'OK, put it in a way that works for you'). The liberal realist would say that this is to misrecognize the nature of human needs. The pragmatist believes that we make our lives impossible by making up impossible choices. In reality we can have, say, justice and mercy, be children and have adult relationships. The liberal realist would say that, often – and particularly in the hard cases, such as, Should we let ex-Nazis lead pleasurable lives? – mercy and justice are compatible only when they lose definition. Both these positions, we can see, are, whatever else they are, different solutions to the same problem: the problem of frustration. The trials and tribulations of wanting are born of frustration; to choose one thing may involve frustrating ourselves of something else. So a lot depends on whether we can bear frustration and whether we want to. If we were creatures less convinced and convincing about our so-called needs we would suffer in quite different ways. Tragedies begin with a person in an emerging state of frustration, beginning to feel the need of something; and at the beginning, for the protagonists, they are not yet tragedies.

Tragedies begin with a dramatic scene in which an urgent frustration unfolds, seeking first definition and then solution. At the very beginning of a tragedy everyone is a pragmatist; people have answers and believe that solutions probably exist. They behave as if they know what frustration is, and that it can be met. But the first English dictionary, Robert Cawdrey's *A Table Alphabeticall* of 1604, has, for the word 'frustrate', 'make voyde, deceive'. 'Make voyde', in seventeenth-century usage, also meant 'to avoid' (as in *Coriolanus*: 'for if / I had fear'd death, of all the men i' the world / I would have 'voided thee' (IV.5), as well as the more familiar meaning of 'to get rid of', 'to empty out'; and 'deceive' in this period meant not only 'to trick' but 'to disappoint'. Avoidance, of course, is a getting rid of, but coupled with the word 'deceive', 'to frustrate' seems to have more to do with lying and cheating than with simply depriving someone of something they need; more to do with guile and cunning and calculation than with meanness. To frustrate someone in this seventeenth-century meaning is to knowingly mislead them. There is something underhand about it, something illicit.

As it happens, Cawdrey was a man, as far as we know,

not given to evasive behaviour, but to plain speaking, a man in trouble with the authorities. He suffered what was for him the tyranny of Elizabeth's established Church (for 'tyrannize' he has in his dictionary 'use crueltie'); he was a Puritan Nonconformist priest who was known for 'speaking divers words in the pulpit, tending to the depraving of the Book of Common Prayer', and 'not conforming himself in the celebration of the divine service and administration of the Sacraments, but refusing to do so' (*The First English Dictionary*) (for 'conform' Cawdrey has 'to make like unto, to consent'). We might now think it entirely appropriate that a future lexicographer would be 'speaking divers words in the pulpit' before losing his living as a priest. 'To frustrate' in Cawdrey's sense is not straightforwardly to refuse someone something; it is, in that strange phrase, to 'make voyde' – literally to make something into nothing, to deceive – literally to cause someone to believe something that is false. It is, one might say, a form of magic, a conjuring trick; something there is not there, something false is true.

In a famous scene in *King Lear* (IV.6) – probably written a year or two after Cawdrey's dictionary – in which Edgar is supposedly helping his blind father, Gloucester, to jump over the cliff, we find again these twinned meanings of a now all-too-familiar word. Unable to deliver himself from torment by suicide, Gloucester invokes the common theme of the play – the loss of props, of cultural forms to contain conflict, the present impossibility of conciliating rival claims; that there are things that can neither be avoided nor banished:

> Alack, I have no eyes.
> Is wretchedness depriv'd that benefit
> To end itself by death? 'Twas yet some comfort,
> When misery could beguile the tyrant's rage,
> And frustrate his proud will.

What you do with proud wills, in both senses, is the play's issue. In the first act Lear, in his tyrant's rage at Cordelia's apparent refusal – and one of the questions the play asks is, in what way is Cordelia frustrating her father? – accuses his daughter of deception: 'Let pride, which she calls plainness, marry her.' Her pride, he says, will have to be her dowry, and get her a husband. Pride means knowing, intractably, what you want. There are many enraged tyrants in this play, and the play keeps working out what we should do with them, and what it is that makes them tyrannical. Gloucester here adds death to the troop of tyrants, but strangely he looks back almost with nostalgia to a time when suicide was an option – even, perhaps alluding to Cleopatra, a noble option – but acknowledging at the same time that the only thing you can do with tyrants is deceive them:

''Twas yet some comfort, / When misery could beguile the tyrant's rage, / And frustrate his proud will.' The point is reiterated; beguiling the tyrant's rage means cheating it, as does frustrating his proud will. Someone is seemingly omnipotent and then, as if by magic, they are not. Their power is void (as is Lear's). It is evidently a paradoxical point that you can cheat the tyrant Death by killing yourself – you win by losing – or by identifying the enemy. Gloucester could deprive Death by dying. In what sense has the tyrant been frustrated?

A tyrant is someone who wants something from us that we don't want to give. And in this sense Death could be described as a tyrant. So we can say, by way of an initial proposal, that a tyrant can be someone we want to frustrate, or even need to frustrate. Our lives (and, indeed, the best lives of others), as Cordelia shows, might depend upon our being able to do this. And given the nature of tyranny, the omnipotence it aspires to, this is going to require some trickery, some invention, some deception. Or, rather, something that can feel like deception only to the one who is being refused. Cordelia is speaking plainly, but to Lear she is speaking with pride; from the tyrant's point of view, not to be given what one wants is indeed to be deceived. And it is a deception because Lear assumes, rightly or wrongly, that it is within Cordelia's power to give him what he wants. A tyrant is someone who believes that what he demands is available and can be given (to be entitled is, by definition, not to question the reality of what it is one is entitled to). So, a familiar situation arises: Cordelia is not deceiving Lear, but Lear feels deceived by her. Cordelia is not giving Lear what he wants, but she is not deceiving him (in her view she would be tricking him if she complied, as her sisters do). In Cawdrey's terms she 'makes voyde' his claim, his demand; Lear feels he is being tricked. What is it to frustrate someone? To make void what they want, but not necessarily to deceive them. What is it to be frustrated? To feel deceived because, it is assumed, the person has whatever it is that you want from them (it is in their gift). This assumption is sometimes true and sometimes not; it would seem more hopeful to assume that they are withholding something that they could give you, but if this turns out not to be true, then your hopefulness is under suspicion (frustration is optimistic in the sense that it believes that what is wanted is available, so we might talk about frustration as a form of faith). When you feel frustrated you are, like Lear, the authority on what you want. If you weren't, you wouldn't be a tyrant and you wouldn't be in a rage.

If you are the frustrator, like Cordelia – the one who in this instance refuses to be complicit with the demand being made, the demand for exorbitant love – you are a different kind of authority; you are the authority on what you are realistically able to give ('I love your Majesty/

According to my bond; no more nor less' (I.1). Or rather, perhaps, the authority on what you want to give. Giving Lear the other thing that Goneril and Regan give him would, we might say, turn her into something she doesn't want to be; would be a way of making a world for herself that she couldn't bear to live in. And put in this way, of course, the frustrator sounds more morally interesting, in a more complex predicament, than the one who is frustrated. Lear is an old man having a tantrum and Cordelia, who will not abide by her father's injunction – 'Mend your speech a little, / Lest you may mar your Fortunes' (I.1) – loses her family in speaking her truth.

And yet there is something symmetrical about Lear and Cordelia; they both, at the beginning of the play, know exactly what they want. And I don't think we solve this problem by saying, in one way or another, that what Cordelia wants is better than what Lear wants. It certainly isn't worse, but it is no less intractable (John Berryman, in *Berryman's Shakespeare*, writes of 'the exquisite matching of a slight excess in Cordelia – an excess of contempt for her sister's extravagant replies over her filial emotion – against a decided prematurity in Lear's ungovernable rage against her'). Lear, we might say, even if it is on the basis of it-takes-one-to-know-one, is not completely wrong in implying that there is something tyrannical – though not enraged – about Cordelia's position. Neither, in the opening scene, can change the other's mind. 'The cause of tragedy,' Stanley Cavell writes in his great essay on King Lear, 'The Avoidance of Love', 'is that we would rather murder the world than permit it to expose us to change' (*Disowning Knowledge*). We would rather destroy everything than let other people change us, so strong is our memory of how changed we were at the very beginning of our lives by certain other people; people who could change our misery into bliss, as if by magic, and which we were unable to do for ourselves (all we could do was signal our distress and hope someone got the point). In the first scene of the first act it is Lear, not Cordelia, who would rather murder the world than expose himself to change. Cavell intimates that we are always looking for an alternative to changing, to being, as he puts it, exposed to change. The frustration scene – which goes back a long way – is the scene of transformation. Everything depends on what we would rather do than change.

To frustrate, then, is to, in one way or another, make void a demand made on oneself; to avoid it or to make it as nothing; and it is to deceive the other person either if you have what they want and won't give it, or if you can create the illusion that you have what they want but are merely refusing to give it. And to be or feel frustrated is to be maddened by having one's demand negated or avoided or tantalized. In this picture it is as though a contract has been broken; as if one person always has what the other person demands of them and the only question is how to get it (God, of course, can be this other person, or the state). In the optimistic version of this story the only question is a pragmatic one: I want to get from A to B, I just have to find out how to get there, and how to get the wherewithal to get there. I want my favourite daughter's love for me declared, so I ask her to speak. This assumes, of course, a preconstituted subject, a person without an unconscious; a person who, because he knows what he wants and needs, knows what he is doing, and so only has to work out how to get his satisfaction; and, if need be, as the Lear story shows, how to bear not getting what is supposedly wanted (it is frustration that makes us inventive, resourceful, at our best and at our worst). Clearly the demand for love, the demand that love be articulated, is something of a special case. As is what can be asked for between parents and children, who are continually having to work out what is possible between them. So the issue of entitlement between parents and children, or between lovers, or between friends, can never be straightforward. The entitled are always too knowing.

Knowing too exactly what we want is what we do when we know what we want, or when we don't know what we want (are, so to speak, unconscious of our wanting, and made anxious by our lack of direction), or when we are so fearful of what we want we displace it on to a known object in a state of militant certainty (if we say that at the beginning of the play Lear is in a terrified state of not knowing what he wants at this stage of his life, or is testing what kingship entails, his reaction to Cordelia's response can be seen in a different light). Knowing what one wants is a way of not exposing oneself to change (or of taking change too much into one's own hands, subjecting it to one's will); and, by the same token, taking up Cavell's point, is prone to make us murderous. So it is tempting to say that we can be at our most self-deceiving in states of frustration; as though frustration were an unbearable form of self-doubt, a state in which we can so little tolerate not knowing what we want, not knowing whether it is available, and not having it that we fabricate certainties to fill the void (we fill in the gaps with states of conviction). The frustration is itself a temptation scene, one in which we must invent something to be tempted by. Satisfaction is no more the solution to frustration than certainty is the solution to scepticism. Indeed, it may be misleading to think of frustration as a question; or it may be a question with no answer; or with only approximate answers, like Lear's 'Tell me, my daughters . . . / Which of you shall we say doth love us most?' (I.1), which reminds us that it is all in the saying, and that the saying is as close as we can get. The play asks us to wonder, in other words, about what we do with our frustration and what our frustration does with us; it being one of the starker facts about the experience of frustration that it raises the question of agency, of whether, quite literally, frustration is something we can do something with, or can ever avoid doing something with. Or whether what we think of as our agency – or our will, or our capacity to make choices – is something invented, called up, by this primal experience of frustration (the idea of the self as a self-cure for our first helplessness in the face of our need, like bravado in a storm). As the British psychoanalyst Wilfred Bion writes in *Second Thoughts*, as we shall see, everything 'depends on whether the decision is to evade frustration or to modify it'.

Frustration is always, whatever else it is, a temptation scene; something we are tempted to get rid of, something we crave false solutions to, something that lures us into the more radical self-deceptions. So there are two propositions I want to consider: first, that the frustrator is always, whatever else she is doing, wanting to change the person she is frustrating (she may drive the person crazy, or away, or be getting someone to face the facts, but a change is being sought; the malign and the benign frustrations are transformative). And second, following on from this, it is extremely difficult to feel one's frustration, to locate, however approximately, what (or who) it might be that one is frustrated by (or about). And there is an obvious, indeed logical, reason why this might matter. Without frustration there can be no satisfaction. Frustration that is unrecognized, unrepresented, cannot be met or even acknowledged; addiction is always an addiction to frustration (addiction is unformulated frustration, frustration too simply met). What, then, is the relationship, the link, the bond, the affinity between frustration and satisfaction? How do we find ourselves fitting them together or joining them up? There may, for example, be something about frustration that makes it resistant to representation, as though our frustrations are the last thing on earth we want to know about. We might prefer spurious frustrations to real satisfactions, or avoid or attack the link between frustration and satisfaction. Frustration, to put it simply, is something we cannot be indifferent to even if indifference can be one of our attempted solutions to it (we pose and boast in the face of our frustrations). The fact that there are frustrations seems to imply, of course, that there are satisfactions, real or otherwise. The fact of frustration has, that is to say, something reassuring about it. It suggests a future.

But it would be sensible to believe that if we have misconstrued the whole notion of frustration – or if our frustrations are difficult to construe – we might have misunderstood the nature of satisfaction: had the meaning but missed the experience. In our frustration we muddle through, or what we do with frustration is make a muddle of it (as if, when it comes to frustration, clarities are available, but not for us). There is, though, one ineluctable fact, one experience that is integral to our development, something that is structural to human relations right from their very beginning; and that is, that if someone can satisfy you they can frustrate you. Only someone who gives you satisfaction can give you frustration. This, one can say, is something we have all experienced, and go on experiencing. You know someone matters to you if they can frustrate you. It was because Lear, as he says so poignantly, 'loved her most' (I.1) that Cordelia most distressed him; and by the end of the play is his most fully realized loss ('Nothing really happens to him,' Barbara Everett writes of Lear in *Young Hamlet*, 'except that he learns that Cordelia actually exists'). It is the satisfaction that leads to frustration which links us to Cawdrey's useful early definition. If the mother, at the start, can make the child feel alive by satisfying his wants, she can, by the same token, make him feel void by her absence; and if the mother is able to make the child feel so good she must surely be deceiving him when she fails to do this. She must be refusing, she must be withholding. Which of them is the tyrant, the mother who doesn't deliver or the frustrated child? What are the preconditions for tyranny? How does it become such a handed-down misery? Does the proud will frustrate, or is it the product of frustration, pride being a state of mind, a way of being organized as a self-cure for certain kinds of frustration? It is to this first deception and making void that we need to turn, with the tyrant's rage and the frustrating of a proud will in mind as one picture of what might be at stake.

The first scene of *King Lear* can't help but make us wonder what the demand for love is a demand for. Lear is asking Cordelia to articulate her love, and it is a kind of deal, both with her suitors and with her father. If she says the right thing she will get a better dowry than her all-too-willing sisters. 'What can you say to draw / A third more opulent than your sisters? Speak.' Cordelia's famous nothings comprise an unwillingness and an inability; there is nothing she wants to say to draw a more opulent third – which would no longer be a third – and nothing she is able to say to such a request. In this drama of excessive demand – excessive from Cordelia's point of view – Lear assumes he knows what she wants, a more opulent dowry than her sisters and all that that entails, and assumes he knows what he wants, her wholehearted cooperation. Her nothings make his demand void, which precipitates his rage and banishment rather than, say, some reconsideration of their respective needs, which in Cavell's terms would be exposure to the possibility of change. Lear's image suggests that Cordelia has a well of desired words that she might draw from for his and therefore her satisfaction. 'The doomed man,' Freud says of Lear in 'The Theme of the Three Caskets' (1916), 'is not willing to renounce the love of women; he insists on hearing how much he is loved.' It is not clear that Lear is contemplating renouncing the love of women rather than, say, enacting something of the symbolic role of king and father; though it is clear why Freud would want to read it this way because he is preoccupied by what modern individuals are doing with and about the love of women. And there is a difference between renouncing the love of women and insisting on hearing how much one is loved. Freud implies in his account that because Lear is approaching his own death, which he in some way experiences as an enforced renunciation of women's love, he insists on hearing about it. Lear can't live without the love of women, and he can't live with the way in which he demands love from them. The demand for love is always a doubt about love; and all doubt begins as a doubt about love.

All love stories are frustration stories. As are all stories about parents and children, which are also love stories, in Freud's view, the formative love stories. To fall in love is to be reminded of a frustration that you didn't know you had (of one's formative frustrations, and of one's attempted self-cures for them); you wanted someone, you felt deprived of something, and then it seems to be there. And what is renewed in that experience is an intensity of frustration, and an intensity of satisfaction. It is as if, oddly, you were waiting for someone but you didn't know who they were until they arrived. Whether or not you were aware that there was something missing in your life, you will be when you meet the person you want. What psychoanalysis will add to this love story is that the person you fall in love with really is the man or woman of your dreams; that you have dreamed them up before you met them; not out of nothing – nothing comes of nothing – but out of prior experience, both real and wished for. You recognize them with such certainty because you already, in a certain sense, know them; and because you have quite literally been expecting them, you feel as though you have known them for ever, and yet, at the same time, they are quite foreign to you. They are familiar foreign bodies. But one thing is very notice-able in this basic story; that however much you have been wanting and hoping and dreaming of meeting the person of your dreams, it is only when you meet them that you will start missing them. It seems that the presence of an object is required to make its absence felt (or to make the absence of something felt). A kind of longing may have preceded their arrival, but you have to meet in order to feel the full force of your frustration in their absence.

You might say, before you met the man or woman of your dreams – or indeed any of the passions of your life – you felt a kind of free-floating diffuse frustration; and what you did by finding the miraculous object was locate the source of your frustration. Falling in love, finding your passion, are attempts to locate, to picture, to represent what you unconsciously feel frustrated about, and by. In this sense we are always trying to find, to get a sense of, what is missing, what we need, what, in Lacan's terminology, we lack. The sources we seek are the sources of our frustration. It would be logical, but only logical, to think – instrumentally, pragmatically, sensibly – that the point of finding out what is missing is to recover it; that at least the first stage of making up for a deprivation is to discover just what it is we are deprived of. That we need to know, or to sense, what we have lost in order to refind it. The finding of an object, Freud says in a famous pronouncement about the erotic life, is always a refinding of an object. And yet Freud also questions – in a way that was taken up by later psychoanalysts – the reality of these lost and found objects. He intimates – and states outright – that we may never have had this object in the first place, and that we can't recover it. That the object, the person we are looking for and can never refind because it never existed, was the wished-for one. We never, in other words, recover from our first false solution to feeling frustrated – the inventing of an ideal object of desire with whom we will never feel the frustration we fear. The ideal person in our minds becomes a refuge from realer exchanges with realer people.

After Freud, psychoanalysts have tended to say, either we did have something – call it the experience of sufficient mothering, the rivalrous pleasures of the Oedipus complex, of competing for the affection of both parents – and we can recover something of that something; and indeed that is what our lives are, a project of recovery and restitution; or we have to ironize our always wanting to get something back that we never had and that never existed anyway (Lacan, in the hyperbolic version of this, said love is giving something you haven't got to someone who doesn't exist). What I think we should be interested in in these accounts is not what they say about love, but what they say about frustration, love's more recondite twin, love's secret sharer. Perhaps what these psychoanalytic stories suggest, at its most minimal, is that there are (at least) four kinds of frustration: the frustration of being deprived of something that has never existed; the frustration of being deprived of something one has never had (whether or not it exists); the frustration of being deprived of something one has had; and, finally, the frustration of being deprived of something one once had, but can't have again. Clearly these forms of frustration flourish in the same hedgerow, and can't always be told apart. But classified, put as starkly, as schematically as this, one thing quickly becomes self-evident: that these are different experiences with different consequences. They bring with them different possibilities, they inspire different futures, they call up different defences, they generate different kinds of unease. And they are applicable to groups, to societies, as well as to individuals. They are also, of course, all contentious. Lear could be said to be suffering from all of them.

Indeed, in terms of the play, or tragedies in general, it may be useful to classify the frustrations as those that turn to revenge – 'to murder the world', as Cavell puts it – and those that do not. Lear is vengeful, though that is not all he is. Cordelia is not; she delivers, Michael Long writes in *The Unnatural Scene*, 'the Desdemona-like speech of resistance which stirs up vengeful repugnances in [Lear]'. There is the frustration that is turned into revenge, for which revenge seems like some kind of solution, and the frustration that is turned to a different kind of account. And this is a story Freud wants to tell; about how the individual's fate is bound up with what he can make out of frustration. In Freud's 'Formulations on the Two Principles of Psychic Functioning' (1911) he reiterates and elaborates on how 'the state of equilibrium in the psyche was originally disrupted by the urgent demands of inner needs'. It is a picture in which the psyche is taken to be in a state of equilibrium, a state of relative balance, until it is disturbed by desire; it is an image if not of violation – what the French psychoanalyst Laplanche famously called the 'attack of the drives on the ego' – then of the creature unsettled by her wanting.

What Freud calls 'the urgent demands of inner needs' means what is called up by a felt sense of frustration, of something needed: 'At this stage,' Freud continues, referring to both the stirrings of desire and, possibly, the baby's early experiences of need,

> whatever was thought of (wished for) was simply hallucinated, as still happens every night with our dream-thoughts. It was due only to the failure of the anticipated satisfaction, the disillusionment, as it were, that this attempt at satisfaction by means of hallucination was abandoned. Instead, the psychic apparatus had to resolve to form an idea of the real circumstances in the outside world and to endeavour actually to change them. With this, a new principle of psychic activity was initiated; now ideas were formed no longer of what was pleasant, but of what was real, even if this happened to be unpleasant. This inception of the *reality principle* proved to be a momentous step.

Freud is describing a simple process: you are hungry, you fantasize a delicious meal, this fantasy doesn't satisfy you, doesn't nourish you or fill you up, and you start working out how in the world you can have this meal that you imagine. You begin by hallucinating, that is, fantasizing, and you end up trying to get the wished-for meal in the real world, which will at best be only an approximation of the one you wanted, but has the advantage of being one you can actually eat. It is the failure of the anticipated satisfaction, its non-arrival once fantasized, that is crucial; it is disillusionment that leads the desiring individual to reality. His first recourse, faced with his frustration, is to attempt to satisfy himself, in fantasy, with a perfect, non-frustrating figure; when this fails, his only recourse is to reality. The failure of an initial wished-for satisfaction leads to the possibility of a more realistic satisfaction. Once satisfaction by means of fantasy breaks down, then, Freud says, the individual has 'to form an idea of the real circumstances in the outside world and to endeavour actually to change them'.

There is a world of difference between erotic and romantic daydream and actually getting together with someone; getting together is a lot more work, and is never exactly what one was hoping for. So there are three consecutive frustrations: the frustration of need, the frustration of fantasized satisfaction not working, and the frustration of satisfaction in the real world being at odds with the wished-for, fantasized satisfaction. Three frustrations, three disturbances, and two disillusionments. It is, what has been called in a different context, a cumulative trauma; the cumulative trauma of desire. And this is when it works.

It is what happens when it doesn't work that prompted Wilfred Bion's theory of thinking; thinking being, in his view, the only way of, as it were, productively working out the inevitable experience of frustration. 'The model I propose,' he writes in *Second Thoughts*,

> is that of an infant whose expectation of a breast is mated with a realization of no breast available for satisfaction [the infant is hungry and no feed is there]. This mating is experienced as a no-breast, or 'absent' breast inside. The next step depends upon this infant's capacity for frustration: in particular it depends on whether the decision is to evade frustration or to modify it. If the capacity for toleration of frustration is sufficient the 'no-breast' inside becomes a thought and an apparatus for thinking it develops. This initiates the state, described by Freud in his 'Two Principles of Psychic Functioning', in which dominance by the reality principle is synchronous with the development of an ability to think and so to bridge the gulf of frustration between the moment when a want is felt and the moment when action appropriate to satisfying the want culminates in its satisfaction. A capacity for tolerating frustration thus enables the psyche to develop thought as a means by which the frustration that is tolerated is itself made more tolerable.

Thought is what makes frustration bearable, and frustration makes thought possible. Thinking modifies frustration, rather than evading it, by being a means by which we can go from feeling frustrated to figuring out what to do about it, and doing it; what Freud called 'trial action in thought' – and what we might call imagination – leading to real action in reality. The ability to think, Bion says, will 'bridge the gulf of frustration between the moment when a want is felt and the moment when action appropriate to satisfying the want culminates in its satisfaction'. And the ability to think also means, and depends upon, the ability to have a conversation. It is, we should note, a gulf between wanting and actually doing something about it; thinking is the link, the bridge, and not an end in itself, as it is when it becomes a bolt-hole of daydream. And the choice, we should also notice, is, in Bion's language, between evading frustration and modifying it. If thinking is the way to modify it, then attacking one's capacity to think would be an evasion; failures of imagination would be the unwillingness to bear with frustration. And Bion is very interested in the ways in which parts of our mind can attack other parts, sabotaging the satisfactions we seek by preventing us finding out what they might be. But what is at stake in these problems and solutions is contact with reality. And reality matters because it is the only thing that can satisfy us. We are tempted, initially, to be self-satisfying creatures, to live in a fantasy world, to live in our minds, but the only satisfactions available are the satisfactions of reality, which are themselves frustrating; but only in the sense that they are disparate from, not in total accord with, our wished-for satisfactions (the most satisfying pleasures are the surprising ones, the ones that can't be engineered). In this picture we depend on other people for our satisfactions. But the quest for satisfaction begins and ends with a frustration; it is prompted by frustration, by the dawning of need, and it ends with the frustration of never getting exactly what one wanted. How could we ever be anything other than permanently enraged?

Perhaps we are permanently enraged, taking revenge on ourselves for not being sufficient for ourselves, and taking revenge on others for never giving us quite what we want. And yet for Bion it is the evading of frustration that is catastrophic. Evasion of frustration, he continues, 'involves the assumption of omniscience as a substitute for learning from experience by aid of thoughts and thinking'. If you can't bear frustration, can't bear the dependence on and involvement of others that satisfaction entails, you have to precipitate yourself into a state of already having and knowing everything (the theological form it takes is, does God need His creation, and if so, how can He be a god if He is in need?). The self-cure for frustration is omniscience, the delusion of omniscience (there must be a figure somewhere who is exempt from frustration, and this is God; we need to be able to imagine someone who doesn't have to feel frustration). Learning from experience means finding ways of making your need compatible with living in the world. Bion thinks we do this by thinking our needs through, observing what the world is like, and trying them out. Finding your place in the world means finding or making a place where your needs work for you.

For Freud and Bion, satisfaction takes thought; we have to digest our frustration before we can digest our food. And the stories they have to tell us are about the struggle for satisfaction, that it doesn't come naturally to us. Indeed, even if we are lucky enough to have had good-enough mothers, good-enough parents, who have helped us contain our frustration and enabled us to think, we are precipitated in this developmental story into the Oedipal world of forbidden desire; the frustrations of the law – our being faced, eventually, with forbidden desires after we have survived the unforbidden ones – follow on from the frustrations inherent in the psychic apparatus's registering and processing of desire. How does anybody ever get any pleasure? Does anybody ever get any pleasure? And if they do, is it worth it? Psychoanalysis tells us that we can understand satisfaction only by understanding frustration, and that we are prone to find frustration unbearable. In this picture, frustration may be the thing that we are least able to let ourselves feel; and by not being able to feel it, to think it, or not being able to feel it or think it enough, we obscure our satisfactions.

To be a little more rigorous-sounding, we could say that our satisfactions are inaccurate, or not as accurate as they might be, or not as satisfying as they might be. Not realistic enough. After all, what pleasures could the omniscient be seeking? To take Bion seriously, if we can't think our frustrations – figure them out, think them through, phrase them – we can't seek our satisfactions. We will have, as they say, no idea what they are.

Neither Freud nor Bion doubt that there are satisfactions to be had; what they do doubt, paradoxically, is our capacity, perhaps our desire, to know what they might be and to try to find them. We should remember Cawdrey's 1604 dictionary definition of 'frustrate', to 'make voyde, deceive'. We frustrate ourselves by what we do to our frustration; we use our frustration to deceive ourselves. We are, at least for Freud and Bion, frustrated of frustration; we empty it out, we evade it. We even avoid it by turning it into a pleasure, or fob ourselves off with pleasures that are knowingly unsatisfying; there is, Freud tells us, a wish to frustrate ourselves that is as strong as any wish we have. But if frustration becomes our pleasure, we are further than ever from satisfaction. Our frustration would seem to be our commonest experience; and yet Freud and Bion show us both how and why there is nothing more opaque about ourselves than our frustrations. That if it is our first nature to need, it is our second nature to obscure our frustration; that we don't want to really think or speak because we don't want to know the nature of, know the experience of, our fundamental frustrations. We prefer our satisfactions without their requisite frustrations. But if it is frustration we hate, it must be satisfaction that we hate even more, because it is only from our sense of frustration that we get a clue about the possibilities of satisfaction. In this sense it is not desire that is the problem but the frustration it discloses. You can't have a desire without an inspiring sense of lack. What we do to our frustration to make it bearable – evade it, void it, misrecognize it, displace it, hide it, project it, deny it, idealize it, and so on – takes the sting out of its tail.

We need to bear with, to know about, our frustrations not simply to secure our satisfactions but to sustain our sense of reality. In the psychoanalytic story, if we don't feel frustration we don't need reality; if we don't feel frustration we don't discover whether we have the wherewithal to deal with reality. People become real to us by frustrating us; if they don't frustrate us they are merely figures of fantasy. The story says something like: if other people frustrate us the right amount, they become real to us, that is, people with whom we can exchange something; if they frustrate us too much, they become too real, that is, persecutory, people we have to do harm to; if they frustrate us too little, they become idealized, imaginary characters, the people of our wishes; if they frustrate us too much, they become demonized, the people of our nightmares. And these, we might say, are two ways of murdering the world: making it impotent or making it unreal. If this was quantifiable we would say that the good life proposed by psychoanalysis is one in which there is just the right amount of frustration. It is, however, rather like Lear's kingdom, not quantifiable. But it seems as though it is all the wrong kinds of frustration that make our lives what they are; that so much depends on what each of us makes of the too much and the too little we get. As Lear says, 'The art of our necessities is strange' (III.2). There are tragic solutions to frustration.

For 'satisfaction' Cawdrey has 'a making amends for wrongs, or displeasures'; it is something, that is to say, to do with justice. If to frustrate was to deceive, to invalidate, to satisfy is to repair a misdemeanour. In a replicate scene, at the beginning of Lear, in which the love between parents and children is in question – 'Lear's shadow is in Gloster,' Yeats wrote in his essay 'The Emotion of Multitude', 'who also has ungrateful children' – Edmund tries to prove his brother Edgar's treachery to their father, Gloucester; to prove it in the guise of attempting to disprove it. Edmund suggests to Gloucester that he will 'place you where you shall hear us confer of this, and by an auricular assurance have your satisfaction' (I.2). We can hear 'oracular' in 'auricular', and Kenneth Muir in his Arden edition glosses the word to give us its religious connotation: 'Shakespeare,' he writes, 'would know the expression "auricular confession".' There is a violation – possibly a desacralizing – of privacy in this treachery; the satisfaction Gloucester will get will not make amends for his suspicion. The satisfaction accruing from the scene will be neither just nor true; nor will it put Gloucester in contact with reality. Satisfaction, here, is one of the forms that frustration takes. One of the ways we frustrate ourselves is through our self-deceiving satisfactions. Gloucester will be frustrated by Edmund's procured satisfaction. One of the ironies, if that is the right word, promoted by Freud and Bion is that many of our satisfactions are forms of frustration. That we are radically inadequate pleasure-seekers because we are unable to countenance our frustration. We are prone to auricular assurances; we fob ourselves off; we are satisfied by privation; we fail to make amends for our frustration. We avoid making better pictures of the exchanges that we seek. True satisfactions, real satisfactions, satisfying satisfactions – it is difficult to know what the phrase is – should be the key to our frustrations, the clue from which can unravel the nature of the felt deprivation.

Even if, as the psychoanalytic story suggests, all

satisfaction is approximate satisfaction – and that is the point and not the problem – frustrations need to be acknowledged. And yet what characterizes what I am calling tragic solutions to frustration is that, almost by definition, they are ineluctable; as if what these darkening tragedies show us is that some frustrations have only tragic solutions; that there are frustrations – or certain people when faced with particular frustrations – that are intractable. And they are intractable because their satisfaction is too exactly imagined. They are frustrations for which no liberating redescriptions are available. As though certain kinds of frustration have their own momentum, their own inner logic. A person who is hungry needs to eat, but not all needs are like hunger; and we may wonder why (or how) they are not. 'Knowledge liberates,' Isaiah Berlin writes in his 'Two Concepts of Liberty', 'not by offering us more open possibilities amongst which we can make our choice, but by preserving us from the frustration of attempting the impossible.' The frustration of attempting the impossible – if such a statement is to be intelligible – may depend more upon our knowledge of frustration than on our knowledge of what is possible. The frustration in attempting the impossible is guaranteed; when it comes to wanting, is there liberating knowledge of what is possible?

Possibility can be born only of experiment, of risk. Both Lear and Gloucester ask their (favourite) children for something – for love and for death – and they are both refused. Both their claims – for special love and assisted suicide – are felt to be impossible by Cordelia and Edgar. Clearly, parents and children want the impossible from each other. This is the tragedy of everyday life. And yet Freud, followed, among others, by Bion, is asking us to imagine something that is seemingly wildly improbable: that there can be only unrealistic wanting, but that unrealistic wanting can be satisfied only by realistic satisfactions; everything else being frustration in disguise, rage and vengefulness, what Cavell calls the murdering of the world. We need, in other words, to know something about what we don't get, and about the importance of not getting it.

On Not Getting It

But how then can you really care if anybody gets it, or gets
what it means, or if it improves them? Improves them for
what? For death? Why hurry them along?

Frank O'Hara, 'Personism: A Manifesto'

No one wants to be the person who doesn't get it.
Doesn't get the joke, doesn't understand what's being
said, what's going on. The 'it', once again, being an
object of desire. Because we want it, we want to get it;
we want the pleasure the joke gives, even if that is the
pleasure of not being amused by it; but either way we
have to get it. What you get when you get it, though,
as jokes make patently clear, is not as obvious as it first
seems; as Freud once remarked, no one ever quite
knows what it is about a joke that amuses them. We
can get pleasure from a joke only when we understand
it, but we don't always understand our understanding.
Here, at least, getting it and not getting it go together.
But mostly, not getting it, whatever it is, means being
left out; left out of the group that does get it, and exempt
from the pleasure that getting it gives.

And yet, André Green – like many, mostly French,
psychoanalysts after Freud – insists in his *Key Ideas for a*

Contemporary Psychoanalysis that we also don't want to get it. There is what Green calls a 'permanent dialectic between misrecognition and recognition in psychic work'; we oscillate between wanting to get it and not wanting to. We can't always afford to be recognized and to recognize ourselves and our needs because of the suffering entailed. To recognize our desire for what it is – as both dependent on others, and forbidden and therefore transgressive – reveals us as too unacceptable to ourselves, too conflicted, too endangered; it puts us, quite literally, at odds with ourselves. It shows us too starkly just how disturbed we can be by our needs. The ego in the Freudian story – ourselves as we prefer to be seen – is like a picture with a frame around it, and the function of the frame is to keep the picture intact. Man, as Green calls us, 'in order to construct an acceptable image of himself, is obliged to deny or misrecognize the essential aspects of it via a process of occultation with a view to avoiding anxiety'. Only the dialectic, the see-saw, between recognition and misrecognition makes things bearable; were we to straightforwardly recognize the essential aspects of ourselves, it is suggested, we would not be able to bear the anxiety. Were we to see our desires all the time as they really are, we would be incapacitated. We are, in actuality, something we don't have the wherewithal to recognize. This is the (psychoanalytic) sense in which we don't get it because we don't want to. The only phobia is the phobia of self-knowledge. In the too-settled and coherent picture of human nature that is psychoanalysis, we are always too daunted by who we are.

And yet we are all too familiar now with the idea that accurate recognition of ourselves and others is both possible and good for us; that we are able to acknowledge our needs and find out whether we have the capacity to meet them. Indeed, consumer capitalism educates us in the virtues and easy pleasures of knowing ourselves and knowing what we want (knowing ourselves meaning simply knowing what we want to have). In this story, self-knowledge is the precondition for satisfaction. And then, in this same culture, we are also encouraged to believe, by psychoanalysis, that such recognition of what we need and want, were it possible, would be something we couldn't tolerate; would, in fact, disclose just how forbidden and discomforting our desires really are. Both stories agree that there is such a thing as self-knowledge available to us, and that self-knowledge is essentially knowledge of our needs and desires. What they disagree about is whether we can stand this self-knowledge, and whether it will make us happy. We can quibble about the whys and wherefores of self-recognition – about which aspect of ourselves we could credit with such capacities, and why we should have these capacities at all – but there is one experience we need little sophistication to recognize, and that is the fundamental, perhaps constitutive, experience of not getting it. We may not know exactly what is lacking in our lives, but we do know the experience of there being something lacking, something missing, something beyond our grasp. We know when there is something we are not getting even if we don't always know what it is. But whatever the 'it' is – the joke, the point, the poem – we would rather get it. And this definite preference is a clue about the ways we want, and the ways we are educated to want.

It is worth remembering that in what is called growing up, not getting it precedes getting it. Our frustration comes before, is the precondition for, our satisfaction. Not getting it precedes getting it; it links us to our losses; and might make us wonder what the early, all-too-literal experiences of not getting it might have been like. Those moments when we did not know that there was an 'it' to get, and so were not not getting it, but doing something else. When getting it was not about knowing what we want, because knowing was not something we were able to do. One of the things I want to consider, then, is what might precede getting it and not getting it; and what, for example, such considerations might have to tell us about jokes, say, or the reading of a poem; or indeed the experience of just listening to people talking, since we begin, as children, by not getting what the adults are on about. In our eagerness to grow up, the pleasures of not getting it, the pleasures, not unmixed, that we started with, are all too easily forgone (the pleasures, for example, of listening to voices without understanding what they are saying). But what might we find ourselves doing if not getting it was the project, not the problem? Not, of course, promising with jokes, which seem to persuade us that there is an 'it' to get, but more promising with works of art, and with people, where it can be a distraction.

Getting it and not getting it keep us in the fold; there is a me who can get it, and an it to be got. It is no longer considered sly to be suspicious of these things, but it's worth seeing whether there are versions of not getting it that are not merely, as they say, the binary opposite of getting it; or that don't link us in strange and evocative ways with some of our earliest experiences. It may at least be worth working out just where – in which realms of experience – not getting it might be a good thing to do. What experiences are made possible by not getting it, and what getting it, whatever it is, might protect us from. Getting what people say, for example, may be complicity, may reveal you are a member of a cult; or colluding with someone to protect yourself from unwanted experiences; or that you prefer agreement to revision or conflict. And this might mean, in this context, not always assuming that there is an it to get; living as if missing the point – having the courage of one's naivety – could also be a point. Not assuming, as

I think we do more often than we realize, that the joke – after God's providential design, and the laws of nature – is our best model of how things work, especially between people. If it had to be formulated, in brief, we could say that the man or woman of your dreams is the person who both gets you and doesn't get you in the way you prefer to be got. That is to say, someone who doesn't treat you only as their favourite joke. Or, everyone is naive all the time.

I want to start, though, in the simpler shallows of a certain version of psychoanalysis; shallow not in the sense of superficial, but in the sense of clear. In many ways it is an account, derived from Freud, that underpins André Green's picture of the nurturing of the acceptable version of the self. 'This theory suggests,' David Malan writes in *Lives Transformed* (co-author Patricia Coughlin Della Selva),

> that anxiety is a signal of the ego, warning of danger or trauma; 'danger' here is any feeling, impulse or action that could threaten the primary bond with caretakers. In other words, any feeling, impulse or action that results in separation from a loved one, or the loss of his or her love, is experienced as threatening, evokes anxiety, and is consequently avoided, giving rise to intrapsychic conflict between expressive and repressive forces within the psyche.

Melding, as much so-called Attachment Theory does, Darwin and Freud – the need to survive through dependent relationships made compatible with the need to be sensually gratified – the developing child's survival depends upon nourishing and protective contact with (the unfortunately termed) 'caretakers'; anything in the individual that disturbs this is potentially life-threatening. So what Green calls the individual's 'acceptable image of himself' is redescribed here as the individual's loveable image of himself (loveable by the caretakers). It is assumed, rightly, in this picture that parenting is a form of aesthetics, that the parents' attention to their child is organized around what is acceptable and unacceptable to them about the child (the myth of unconditional love is there to conceal this). The parents want to keep their child as 'beautiful' as possible, that is, they want their feelings about the child to be as beautiful (that is, acceptable) as possible – and this is something that the child has to of necessity collude with; but the child is also something else, something out of the orbit of the parents' desire (in this sense growing up is a quest for illegitimacy). The familiar, and indeed salient, example Malan gives is of anger. 'If a child is consistently punished for the expression of anger,' he continues,

> he will begin to get anxious when angry and will learn ways to avoid its expression. Let's say that passivity and

withdrawal become the child's strategies of choice for avoiding the experience and expression of anger (and its feared consequences). Eventually, he may retreat to this position so automatically that even he is unaware of feeling angry inside. The defences come to *replace* the feeling itself and can result in character pathology (e.g., passive aggressive or avoidant personality disorders), affecting all future relationships.

This, one could say, is a story of the genesis of someone not getting it, of a person over time not recognizing their feelings; they experience themselves as withdrawn or passive or blank when they are in fact angry; and so, by the same token, making it impossible for the other person to recognize what they are feeling – I experience you as a shy person when you are in fact someone who desires me or loathes me. Not getting it is here conceived of as an essential, self-protective project; the consequence of it – of this evolving solution to disruptive feeling – is an estrangement from what Malan calls an 'emotional core'. Real feeling is replaced by defences against it, and the defences come to seem to be what one is really feeling (all these stories depend on there being feelings that can be identified as real). Not getting it here means not getting emotional contact with yourself and others; feeling ceases to be the medium of contact and exchange between people, but becomes an intricate system of unassuaging evasions. One is doubly left out, from one's so-called emotional core and from other people; unpaid on both sides. This is clearly a recognizable and dismaying picture; and it works round a simple idea: the idea of replacement. Feelings, desires, beliefs, thoughts and actions can be literally replaced, put in the place of, substituted for and sacrificed to, the defences against them. I am cross: it threatens to spoil the relationship I depend on: I make myself, I turn myself, into a nice, kind, gentle person. In this psychic alchemy, this magical act, this disappearing act, I reappear as acceptable to others, and therefore to myself (that is the logical order here). And what happens to the anger? It comes out as what are called 'symptoms', prevailing forms of unease. Symptoms, in this sense, are obscured communications.

There are several things worth noting here; first, that the parents are unable to get, to bear or bear with, the full range of their child's emotional life. They don't want to engage with it, they want to exclude it from the frame. And the child, who is absolutely dependent on their love and goodwill, has to be an accomplice to their aesthetic in order to survive. The child has to get what it is that the parents want from him, what they need him to be. The child, in this picture, is in an odd position; he has got what it is that the parents want from him – in this instance, not to be angry. But the parents cannot get, in the fullest sense, that the child is angry and needs to be.

The child is taken to be good at recognizing (the parents' needs), but deprived of sufficiently good experiences of being recognized. The child is the unrecognized recognizer. If you want, as Freud suggests, to re-create, to recover, your relationship with your parents, it is always going to be a quest for selective recognition. You will be attentive to the needs of the other person, and they will see in you only what they want to see. You must sacrifice being recognized for recognizing. Your project, so to speak, is to fit in with what the other wants you to be (or what you imagine they want you to be); but there are aspects of yourself that are always threatening to break the bonds you need. We are accomplices struggling to become collaborators – at least in this picture. We make ourselves out of the demands others make of us, and out of whatever else we can use.

What we get, fundamentally, is what the (essential) other needs us to be; this is where we start from. Getting it as an estranging collusion. Not getting it, in this first, formative drama, puts one at mortal risk; giving up on getting it, as a way of being, at least in this context, seems inconceivable. And yet if we move from the modern Freudian and post-Freudian aesthetics of mothering (and parenting) – the story of parenting as a (largely unconscious) attempt at sorting out the acceptable and the unacceptable in the developing child – to the aesthetics of modernist art and its contemporary versions, there is one discernible thread that turns up rationalized as theory, or pronounced as prejudice; and this is the project of making art that the audience don't get, or even can't get (the task of modern art, the social critic Theodor Adorno wrote in *Aesthetic Theory*, is 'to make things of which we do not know what they are'.) As though to get some things, to be able to give a fluent account of them, is to misrecognize their nature; to pre-empt the experience by willing the meaning, or by supposedly articulating the meaning. Meaning is imposed wherever experience is disturbing; which is why the psychoanalyst – another 'modernist' artist – wants to talk about what the patient says, not what he means. The audience cannot work out what the artist needs or wants from them; and that may be the point, the artist herself may not know. Either not getting it becomes, in the glib sense, getting it ('the worse your art is,' the poet John Ashbery remarked, 'the easier it is to talk about'); or, in the audience being actively prevented from getting it, something else becomes possible in relation to it. Not being able to find out what the writer wants from the reader – exhausting the possibilities of the reader getting it – forces the reader, if he is sufficiently intrigued, to do something else.

The shallow psychoanalytic account reported above, provides, reassuringly perhaps, the parent, the child, and ourselves as readers, with something to recognize, something to get; in the example cited, it is what is taken to be the underlying anger. We could say, with this example in mind, that parenting is a good setting for the idea of accurate recognition – children have irreducible essential needs that need to be discerned and responded to by 'caretakers', though these needs become more complicated over time (there is what D. W. Winnicott calls 'the imaginative elaboration of physical function', and we might call culture). And recognition will inevitably be patchy, and not always felt to be sufficient. And children will always need to try to satisfy their parents, to become what they assume the parents need, and find themselves both unwilling and unable to do this. (No child ever recovers from not having cured his parents.) But what happens if we draw a line from the parent and child in this formative and familiar drama of getting it and not getting it to the adult the child will become and the objects in the cultural field that begin to engage her. And then ask a simple question: why is it so difficult to enjoy not getting it? How does the child resist, what else can the child do, if anything, other than try to get it? And what happens to that aspect of the adult that doesn't get it, and doesn't want to? The adult, whose naivety may be the most important, the most original, thing about him?

If the line 'He didn't get it' turned up in, say, a John Ashbery poem – in a contemporary poem of sentences apparently unmoored from context, of words at a remove from their obvious referents – we would assume that the 'it' was either a joke, a contagious illness or a communication that eluded him. It could be an accusation, or the description of a piece of luck (or bad luck). But at its most minimal it would usually refer to someone being unable, or perhaps unwilling, to join in (not getting it has everything to do with insiders and outsiders). Groups of people tend to be defined, or to define themselves, by the things they all get. Outsiders don't get it, and if or when they do, it is a shock to the system (as all immigrants know). Such moments of recognition, when connections are suddenly sprung – when something is said that is something in common – always promise an abundance; they seem to push on an open door. They can be moments of falling in love or falling in league, of affinity or solidarity, of assimilation or conspiracy (in *Othello*, a play very much about insiders and outsiders, we can see Iago as a man helping someone to get something that they do and don't want to get). We have been educated to think of language, and of people, as something we can get, and in what might be called the fullest sense of the word. Getting it, or not getting it – both the experience, which is acute, and the phrase, which seems not to be – reminds us of the investment we are brought up to have in understanding as a measure of intimacy and competence; and of how hard a word 'understanding' is to understand. The understanding between people supposedly referring to some shared foundations, or to what might be underneath where we stand. 'Getting it' means something understood even if we can't always, or even often, give an account of what has been understood, or indeed of what this understanding involves (we might want Othello to tell us how he has come to his understanding of Desdemona through his understanding of Iago). When we talk of getting it – the joke, the point, the work of art – we need to be aware of the anxieties that collusion apparently spares us, and of the terrors and treats of there being no discernible connection between people.

If getting it gives us some kind of pleasure, what are the pleasures of not getting it, of being, as we say, left out or in the dark, or clueless? It can be humiliating not to get it – indeed, I want to suggest that humiliation is always a form of not getting it, and that humiliation sheds a unique and horrifying light on what not getting it might be about. But I also want to suggest that we are under considerable pressure to get it; that, in the language of psychoanalysis, it is a super-ego command – one of the most intimidating in what is a horrible repertoire – that dominates our lives: *'You must get it'* (you must get it in order to qualify as a member of our group). We need to imagine what a life would be like in which this command had been dropped, a life in which there was nothing to get because what went on between people, what people wanted from each other, couldn't possibly be phrased in that way. Our lives would not be about getting the joke or the point. Or, to put it slightly differently, there would be other pleasures than the pleasures of humiliation.

Children are people who don't get it, until they do; so we might have to consider what is lost, what has to be given up, in the struggle to get it, the struggle that once you have got it feels like no struggle at all. Getting it, as we shall see, means not being humiliated (or not recruiting the 'it' to diminish you); and is, perhaps by the same token, perhaps not, among our greatest pleasures; or at least gives us the greatest sense of relief. A lot is at stake in our getting it, a lot hangs on it. When I do get it, it is as if I have triumphed over my abject insufficiency; when I don't get it I am left with . . . What? This chapter is about what we are left with when we don't get it. It is, after all, not an uncommon experience, but not one routinely sought. It is not illogical to think that if you don't get it – at least, say, when one is being educated – you should try to get it, rather than do something else. Not getting it all too easily, in certain situations, programmes you, instructs you to do what you can to get it. And clearly there is a difference between not getting how the electoral system works and not getting *The Waste Land*. But how, it is worth wondering, would you teach someone to not get it? What would that be like teaching them to do; teaching someone how not to swim, how not to ride a bike, how not to understand what people are saying to them? Teaching them how not to conform without trying not to conform? Teaching them forms of appreciation that require neither defiance nor compliance? To get all, or some of this, I want to start with getting it, and what it does for us, and what it can't do.

In my first job as a child psychotherapist I worked as a consultant to the staff of what was then called a School for Maladjusted Children; in those days – the late 1970s and early 1980s – that meant all the children they didn't know what to do with who were not yet in prison or hospital. It was extremely distressing and inspiring work to teach in these schools; and so the teachers were offered an hour a week to talk to me about anything they wanted to talk about. It was entirely voluntary, and the teachers could use it as supervision or as some kind of personal therapy. One of the first people who came to see me was the art teacher – a man in his forties who later described himself to me as 'not an ex-hippy but a hippy' – who came into my room and sat in a not uncomfortable silence for about ten minutes, and then said to me, as if out of huge rumination, 'If you look after me who will look after you?' I asked, 'Did you have to do a lot of looking after when you were growing up?' And he replied, as though we were in the middle of a long conversation, 'Yes, my mother was sick a lot, and my dad was away.' And I said, for no apparent reason, 'When you were looking after your mother, did anything really strange ever happen, anything you just didn't get?' There was a pause, and he said, 'Often, very often, when I was getting up to fill the coal scuttle downstairs, my mother would shout down from her bedroom, "Can you fill the coal scuttle" . . . so I never know whether I'm doing it because I want to or because she's telling me to.' I remarked, 'You said "know" as if it's still happening now,' and he replied, 'It is happening now because I never really know if I'm doing what I want or whether I'm acting under instruction.' I asked, 'Is coming to see me an example of this?' and he smiled and said, 'Yes, and I think I'll go now.' He got up, walked towards the door, and as he opened it he said to me, 'I am going back to my bean-field'; and I had this tremendously powerful feeling of affection for him, as if he had understood me, *Walden* having been an important book in my life, though he had no way of knowing this. (In Jack Tizard's obituary for the psychoanalyst and paediatrician D. W. Winnicott, he wrote that it wasn't the case that Winnicott understood children, but that they understood him.) I felt profoundly understood at that moment and felt sure, as turned out to be true, that something had happened between us that promised a future; that something had begun that we would both want to continue.

The first paragraph of Chapter 7, 'The Bean-Field', in Henry David Thoreau's *Walden* begins:

> Meanwhile my beans, the length of whose rows, added together, was seven miles already planted, were impatient to be hoed, for the earliest had grown considerably before the latest were in the ground; indeed they were not easily to be put off. What was the meaning of this so steady and self-respecting, this small Herculean labor, I knew not. I came to love my rows, my beans, though so many more than I wanted. They attached me to the earth, and so I got strength like Antaeus. But why should I raise them? Only Heaven knows. This was my curious labor all summer – to make this portion of the earth's surface, which had yielded only cinquefoil, blackberries, johnswort, and the like, before, sweet wild fruits and pleasant flowers, produce instead this pulse. What shall I learn of beans or beans of me?

'Our mind is chanced, but not forced, by language,' Stanley Cavell remarks in *The Senses of Walden*, his commentary on the book. I felt fortunately chanced but not forced by the possibility of a shared language; the art teacher's parting remark making me feel, as it were, that we both spoke *Walden*. It was very clear to me when he made the remark, on leaving, how pertinent that chapter was to our discussion, even though I could not recall, in detail, the actual writing. He looks after his mother, I look after him; Thoreau looks after his beans, but what makes him do it – 'But why should I raise them?' (raising as in raising children). The beans, the raising of them, 'attached me to the earth', that is, Mother Earth; got him 'strength like Antaeus'; but there was something Thoreau didn't get: 'What was the meaning of this so steady and self-respecting, this small Herculean labor, I knew not.' The 'small Herculean labor' of filling the coal scuttle also had an enigma in it, and it was to do with knowing; 'I never know', he said, when he might have said, 'I never knew'. The question is not simply, why am I doing this? It is also the less metaphysical question – the question that begins in the family – who am I doing this for, and what, in doing this, am I doing for them? 'What shall I learn of beans or beans of me?' ('I did not read books the first summer,' Thoreau remarks, 'I hoed beans', the implied question being, what do books learn from our reading of them?) The art teacher is called to do something that he is already doing, and he doesn't get it, and not getting it here means being confounded, being undone, being diminished, by his mother's words; he is left feeling that his agency, or rather his desire, is confused or compromised, or even stolen from him; he thought he was doing something good that he wanted to do – 'steady and self-respecting . . . labor', in Thoreau's words – but perhaps he was merely acting under orders, perhaps he was just a part of his mother's body – one of her limbs – or had no privacy.

Not getting this coincidence of his mother's words and his actions was a formative anguish for him; his getting me, whether or not it was his intention – and my guess is that it was an unconscious probe to find out which group I belonged to, which gang I was in – was a formative link. His reference to *Walden* made me feel we had a shared world. Both experiences you will notice are fantasies of understanding, what we might call the promise of knowing things in common; though it would be difficult to describe what kind of experience this knowing was, or indeed whether it was a kind of knowledge. The art teacher needs to know, to understand, what is going on between him and his mother (and in terms of what might be going on between me and him); I might think that I don't need to know what's going on between him and me because in speaking *Walden* we seem to be on the same page, even though we are quite different people and have only just met. In both cases, though, the opportunities for collusion, for the disavowal of our myriad of differences, are as great, one might say, as the promises of affinity. Sharing is a bind as well as a boon. We get each other, through *Walden*, which might release us, as it in fact did, into a shared future; and he believes that if he can get what was going on between him and his mother in those moments, he might be free of her, and freer to act, to desire. Not getting it is humiliating; getting it is the opposite. What is the opposite of humiliation? Or, to put it a little more pragmatically, what are the alternatives to humiliation; what are our options?

There is abandonment, in Cavell's sense of 'feeling enthusiastically what there is to abandon yourself to'. We are humiliated, that is to say, when we entrust ourselves or are entrusted to people who don't care for our well-being; people who need to render us helpless, people who need us to feel humiliated. People who abandon us when we abandon ourselves to them. Not getting it, at its worst, is a malign helplessness; what we need in these situations is not so much a room of one's own, but a gang of one's own. The dream of like-mindedness is a dream about a group of people, or a couple, in which the possibility of not getting it – indeed the whole issue of not getting it – has disappeared.

Perhaps what is being referred to is a time before getting it and not getting it was the issue, or was at issue. So we might consider what it would be to live a life in which getting it is not always the point, in which there is nothing, to all intents and purposes, to get; and our picture of this can be, in adult life, when we are lost in thought, absorbed in something without needing to know why we are absorbed, or indeed what we are absorbed in; or when we dream. Or, going back to the life of the infant, the life before jokes, before language, which is a life sponsored by somebody who has to be able to get it, that is, to imagine the baby's needs, to imagine what will assuage the infant's distress. And here we can see, if we take infancy as some kind of basic or informing picture, or just as a useful analogy, that someone is free not to have to worry about getting it or not getting it, so long as someone else is doing that for them, or trying to. This is the not getting it that depends upon the other person getting it; we might say, the infant doesn't know that he is telling the mother something, or that he is telling the mother a joke; but she has to live as if he is telling her something, which could be like a joke, that she can get. The mother gets a joke, and gets a joke that is not being told.

For the infant there is nothing to get, that is, to understand, and for the mother there is something to get. If the mother doesn't get it – can't apprehend the infant's need – the child may never get the opportunity to know that there is something to get, something about him, call it his need, that he needs someone else to get (he will, as we say, have no sense of humour, he won't get the joke because he won't even know it is a joke). We don't think of babies as having to get it in order to join in, but we can think of mothers having to get what their infants need. Mothers are supposed to know; and this, of course, puts great pressure on mothers. However well they get their babies, they can't always get what their babies need.

That is to say, they inevitably allow the baby the experience of having a mother who doesn't get it; and in which the not getting it, ideally, is not catastrophic. Only the idealized mother – the perfect, wished-for mother in the child's mind – always gets it. There is, in other words, a freedom – a freedom from the tyranny of perfection – in not understanding and in not being understood (understanding is not always the best thing we can do with need). All tyrannies involve the supposedly perfect understanding of someone else's needs.

So there is something perhaps more difficult to conceive of, sometimes born of resignation and sometimes not – a life in which not getting it is the point and not the problem; in which the project is to learn how not to ride the bicycle, how not to understand the poem. Or, to put it the other way round, this would be a life in which getting it – the will to get it, the ambition to get it – was the problem; in which wanting to be an accomplice didn't take precedence over making up one's own mind. As though the will to understand – our second nature, as it were – was sometimes a distraction from, or an evasion of, something more valuable or even more pleasurable. It might be like suddenly realizing that we had been given the wrong map, the wrong set of instructions; that, say, instead of our owing each other something it dawned on us that we could do something else together. And putting it like this, of course, reminds us that the wish not to get it might be akin, at least in some versions, to what Lacan calls our 'passion for ignorance' and what Freud described, rather less grandly, as our wish not to know about the things that we suffer from (as though not knowing about them diminishes our suffering, which is a tribute in itself to our investment in knowing). Not getting it could just be determined avoidance; being taught how not to get jokes could just be a surreal dystopian vision. It could be a kind of longing, in which satisfaction is felt to be the spoiler of desire, or food the saboteur of hunger. But what I want to promote here is the alternative or complementary consideration; that getting it, as a project or a supposed achievement, can itself sometimes be an avoidance; an avoidance, say, of our solitariness or our singularity or our unhostile interest and uninterest in other people. From this point of view we are, in Wittgenstein's bewitching term, 'bewitched' by getting it; and that means bewitched by a picture of ourselves as conspirators or accomplices or know-alls. In this picture, once we are lucky enough to have developed into people for whom getting it and not getting it are the issue, we might then want to learn not getting it, or unlearn the supposed need to be the kind of people who always get it; who get the joke whether or not they find it funny; who get the poem whether or not they think it is a good one; who get the point so they are in a position to evaluate it. What would the community of those who didn't get it be like? What kind of consensus would they be capable of?

Not getting it might be described here as a determined, tenacious ignorance that is in the service of something better, something better than complicity; not an innocence or a faux naivety but a belief, for example, that in some situations not getting it is more revealing and getting it is more obscuring; that we can be fobbed off by satisfactions of getting it and oddly enlivened by the perplexity of not getting it. From this perspective you could say, for example, if you understand why you are with the person you are with, then you are not really with them; you could say that the belief that there are consensual objects of desire is an anxiety about objects of desire, about the unfathomable idiosyncrasy of desiring or an anxiety about there not being any objects of desire. You could say, more obviously, if you get *Othello* you have no idea of what it is about (the question is whether you have something to say about *Othello*, or are aware of there being something you can't say, not whether you get it). And you could also say, perhaps less obviously, that if you want to be with somebody who gets you, you prefer collusion to desire, safety to excitement (sometimes good things to prefer but not always the things most wanted). We have been taught to wish for it, but the wish to be understood may be our most vengeful demand, may be the way we hang on, as adults, to our grudge against our mothers; the way we never let our mothers off the hook for their not meeting our every need. Wanting to be understood, as adults, can be, among many other things, our most violent form of nostalgia.

There is, in other words, a difference between somebody saying something that makes one feel understood and somebody saying something striking. There is, or there can be, a difference between reading something intelligible and reading something that has a powerful effect; between words as procurers of experiences and words as consolidators of knowledge. There is a difference between the wish to comfort and assuage and the wish to provoke and unsettle. And we speak to each other and read for both these opportunities, and for other experiences as well. But it is the linguistic arts that seem at once hospitable to the notion of intelligibility, and in which intelligibility can be put into more or less intelligible question.

This essential perplexity is highlighted in the contrasting aims of psychoanalytic treatment, in the question of cure; is the aim of psychoanalytic treatment to increase the person's understanding of herself or to free her to desire? And are these aims complementary, inextricable from each other, or mutually exclusive? Does my understanding of my so-called self free my desire or inhibit it? Does it, in William James's words, allow for 'novelty and possibility forever leaking in'? Is the good life one in which I get it – get, to some extent, what's going on inside me and in others, get who I am – or one in which I don't need to, one in which the examined life is unliveable? One definition of a psychoanalytic cure, for example, might be a new-found freedom to ironize any description of oneself: or, the newfound freedom to work out what we want to give to other people, not what we supposedly owe them. So, have we constructed a picture of the self made for understanding – to appease our desire for understanding – just as one might write a poem, be taught to write a poem, made for literary criticism? What would it be to be a person whom no one could easily describe, or whom no one could come up with a description of that seemed pertinent or useful or illuminating? When we meet one of these people – and we are more likely to meet them in fiction in the novels, say, of Dostoyevsky than in the novels of Jane Austen – it exposes the tacit knowledge, the tacit assumption, that we tend to live by; that there are many people whom we think we do more or less get, or whom we get enough not to have to worry about it. It is of course a question of some consequence, what we do with, what we want from, people we don't get. In universities this is called the history of madness, or anthropology (and used to be called theology). We have psychiatric diagnoses to ensure that there are no people we don't get.

In the smaller world of literary criticism, and the

larger world of so-called popular culture, this is known as the 'difficulty' of modern poetry. If, at least as a reader of poetry, your project is not to get it, you are better off reading John Ashbery than Philip Larkin, J. H. Prynne rather than John Betjeman. Getting it is for what Geoffrey Hill in *Critical Writings* calls the 'community of initiates'. When Ashbery was asked in an interview why his poetry was so difficult, he replied that when you talk to other people they eventually lose interest, but that when you talk to yourself, people want to listen in. No one, other perhaps than Ashbery, talks to themselves in the way he writes poetry; but what Ashbery is suggesting in his whimsically shrewd way is that the wish to communicate estranges people from each other. If you talk to people, he suggests, they lose interest; if you ignore them – or, rather, if you ignore them by talking to yourself – they are engaged. As though curiosity might sometimes be preferred to consolation, listening in or overhearing preferred to communication or comprehension. The wish to understand or be understood – to, as we say, communicate or be accessible – might give a false picture, might be a hiding place, might be a retreat or a refuge.

The phrase 'not getting it' has in it the idea that you might get it; while the other possibility is that there is not an 'it' to get; that a person or a poem are not in that sense gettable, as if we can have the wrong picture of both objects, and then have to take all the consequences that

that wrong picture involves. To put it at its simplest, the famous difficulty of modern poetry is one form that a modern scepticism took about what it is to understand; about what we might be doing or wanting in the act of understanding. What do you say about a poem – or about and to a person – if the project is not to understand, if the intention is to not get it? If you don't want intelligibility, what do you want instead? Do you stop using the word 'understanding' and start using the word 'redescription'? Do you give an account that does not aspire to be an explanation? Infants and young children have to be, in a certain sense, understood by their parents; but perhaps understanding is one thing we can do with each other – something peculiarly bewitching or entrancing – but also something that can be limiting, regressive, more suited to our younger selves; that can indeed be our most culturally sanctioned defence against other kinds of experience – sexuality being the obvious case in point – that are not subject to understanding, or which understanding has nothing to do with, or is merely a distraction from. That if growing up might be a quest for one's illegitimacy, this is because one's legitimacy resides in what one thinks one knows about oneself. This, I think, is what Freud quickly discovered and then tried to undiscover. It is not an increase in self-knowledge that Freud describes, but its limits. He tells us a story about the need to grow out of a need for understanding and being understood. The child needs his parents to get him – to be sufficiently attentive to his needs and fears – and then he needs to be weaned of this. Understanding first – by definition, within reason – then the freedom to also not understand, or need to. Psychoanalysis is, in fact, the treatment that weans people from their compulsion to understand and be understood; it is an 'after-education' in not getting it. Through understanding to the limits of understanding – this is Freud's new version of an old project. Freud's work is best read as a long elegy for the intelligibility of our lives. We make sense of our lives in order to be free not to have to make sense.

Psychoanalysis, at its inception, promised its disciples apparently unprecedented opportunities of comprehension and explanation. And yet quite quickly it began to sound like *Shakespeare Made Easy*, the 'unique series' of bilingual editions of Shakespeare's plays that, as Slavoj Žižek describes it in *Enjoy Your Symptom!*, has 'the original archaic English on the left page and the translation into common contemporary English on the right page'; 'the obscene satisfaction provided by reading these volumes,' Žižek writes, 'resides in how what purports to be a mere translation into contemporary English turns out to be much more . . . "To be or not to be, that is the question", becomes something like, "What's bothering me now is: shall I kill myself or not?"' What Žižek calls the 'obscene satisfaction' of these translations – akin to what psychoanalytic interpretations can sound like to their critics – is the sheer bathos of their banality; to understand here is reductive in the sense of reducing in complexity. Shakespeare is made easy in so far as ease is all that is wanted. There is no pleasure in the language resisting what we might want to do with it; and no assumption that the pleasures of resistance may be desired. For Žižek the 'standard remakes' of Hitchcock films are 'something like' *Hitchcock Made Easy* because 'although the narrative is the same, the "substance", the flair that accounts for Hitchcock's uniqueness, evaporates'. And yet, Žižek intimates, it may be part of the 'obscene satisfaction' of *Shakespeare-and-Hitchcock Made Easy* that we can't help but wonder, through all this unwitting parody, about the so-called uniqueness of our masters; of what we are getting when we think we get them, of how we recognize these poor substitutes, which give us pleasure, which certainly don't make Shakespeare and Hitchcock seem too clever, that is, cleverer than us. 'Or what if this uniqueness is a myth,' Žižek writes,

the result of our (spectators') transference, elevation of Hitchcock into The Subject Supposed To Know? What I have in mind is the attitude of overinterpretation: everything in a Hitchcock film has to have a meaning – there are no contingencies – so that when something doesn't fit, it's not his fault, but ours – we didn't really get it.

What Žižek is exercised by here is what we, as readers and spectators, have conferred upon Shakespeare and Hitchcock; we have attributed to them a kind of omniscience, a super-knowledge, which lures us into what Žižek calls 'the attitude of overinterpretation'. We assume their absolute knowledge of what they are doing so that anything that doesn't make sense we didn't get (we are desperate to have an affinity with them, to be their accomplices). When there is a 'Subject Supposed to Know' – the position conferred upon the psychoanalyst by the patient, according to Lacan – there is a subject supposed not to, a subject, in Žižek's words, who 'didn't really get it'. But someone does really get it. And this binds us, in a very particular way, to Shakespeare's texts, Hitchcock's films (and to our parents and lovers and analysts, and all our other specialists). If knowledge, if getting it, is the currency, they are indispensable, we can't remake them, translate them or possibly even redescribe them; what is exposed is the fantasy of purity in play, and the insufficiencies created. In this familiar division of labour there is a plenitude – the one who, because he is supposed to know, is in the know – and there is an inadequacy: parents and children, teachers and students, Shakespeare and us.

Once knowing is the issue, distance opens up; the distance between Hamlet's soliloquy and the rewrite is ridiculous; the distance between Hitchcock's original films and the contemporary remakes is dispiriting. Everything we value – in Žižek's terms, the 'uniqueness', the 'substance', the 'flair' – seems to fall into the gap between them. This gap is created by the notion of getting it. And in its malign version it is what psycho-analysts call a sadomasochistic contract; the masochist says, 'You can do what you like to me as long as you never leave me (indeed, the worse the things you do to me are, the more I know you will never leave me)'; and the sadist says, 'I can do what I like to you because we both know that you will never leave me (indeed, my doing what I like to you is proof that you will never be able to leave).' The one who is supposed to know – the one who has supposedly got it, in both senses – torments the other one who is supposed not to know. But if knowledge was not at stake, what would be the issue? Certainly in this picture, the common theme, knowledge or the lack of it, is what holds people together; and without considerable cruelty – the cruelty entailed by supposi-tions of knowledge – it is implied that people would not be held together, or would not be kept together in the same way, with the same ends in view.

There is a link, coming from childhood, between aban-donment, in both senses, and lack of knowledge. What Žižek calls 'the attitude of overinterpretation' is a self-cure for the fear of what I am calling 'not getting it'. Over-interpretation is getting it with a vengeance. It betrays an anxiety, so to speak, of not being close enough to, not being of the same mind as, the one supposed to know. As though well-being, or even survival, was a function of closeness, and closeness was a function of knowledge (closeness means wanting to be close to those who know, especially to those who seem to know us). Knowledge, Freud tells us, is of absence; it is the way we measure distance. If overinterpretation is the rather frantic desire to be as close as possible, scepticism may be deemed to be, whatever else it is, a wariness, a suspicion, about what we might be up to – what we might be wanting to put out of our minds – through our so-called knowledge of other minds; scepticism being not just a doubting of what we can know about others, but a doubting of the value of such knowledge, and therefore a broached imagining of what knowing might prevent or preclude us from experiencing with each other. 'His critics have for the most part made their contemporaries less that they might make Shakespeare more,' Thoreau wrote in his *Journal* of 1842.

There is a strange line in Act I, scene 3 of *Othello* in which after lengthy and eloquent accounts by Othello, and rather more reticent and underplayed accounts by Desdemona, of their love for each other, Desdemona's outraged and frantic father, Brabantio, bails out in wrathful resignation. Brabantio, in effect, hands the couple over to the state and suggests that the state, as represented by the Duke of Venice, continue with its business; and he hands the couple over to each other, but with a warning about parents and children:

> God be wi' you! I have done
> Please it your grace, on to the state affairs.
> I had rather to adopt a child than get it.
> Come hither, Moor:
> I here do give thee that with all my heart
> Which, but thou hast already, with all my heart
> I would keep from thee. For your sake, jewel,
> I am glad at soul I have no other child:
> For thy escape would teach me tyranny,
> To hang clogs on them. I have done, my lord.

'I had rather to adopt a child than get it.' For 'adopt' the *Oxford English Dictionary* has 'to take voluntarily into any relationship (1548) . . . to take up from another and use as one's own (1607) . . . to christen or rechristen (1601)'. 'Get it', of course, means 'begetting' – there are many images in the play of malign procreation – but also has our contemporary meaning of 'understanding' and 'capture'; the *OED* has 'to gain . . . win . . . acquire' in Middle English, and 'to learn, commit to memory (1582) . . . to find out, obtain as a result, by calculation or experiment (1559) . . . to catch, contract an illness (1601)'. In *Shakespeare Made Easy* terms, Brabantio is saying something like 'I would rather choose a child than produce one'; but he is also contrasting adopting a child and understanding one, because he certainly can't get, that is, comprehend how Desdemona could, as he sees it, do such a thing to him or to herself as desire Othello. If she was an adopted child, would this whole thing make more sense (Othello, of course, having been adopted by the state)?

Brabantio is glad he doesn't have another child because if Desdemona's behaviour, her 'escape', as he calls it, 'would teach me tyranny, to hang clogs on them', meaning, as Michael Neill glosses it in the Oxford World's Classics edition of the play, 'shackle them to heavy logs of wood to prevent their escape (as practised with slaves as well as animals)'. If you get your children they won't escape, they will be like animals and slaves and never leave. To get a child, in both senses, is supposed to mean ownership. Within two hundred lines, in the last soliloquy of the scene, Iago will be saying of Cassio, and by extension Othello himself, that he will 'get his place and to plume up my will / In double knavery'. Getting his place puns on knowing his place, and how that very knowing can lead to the displacement of rivals. Brabantio has lost his place (in Desdemona's affections), and Iago is determined to win what he thinks of as his place. 'Getting' is associated for both of them with acquisitiveness, and begetting with, as psychoanalysts would say, controlling their objects: 'I had rather to adopt a child than get it': 'I would prefer that she was nothing really to do with me'; 'If I had known what happens to one's children, what they do to you, I would have adopted one instead' (the adopted perhaps being more like slaves and animals). Brabantio is at a loss, though the scale of his loss is not yet evident.

If you adopt a child is it evident that you are less likely to get it, to understand it; or is consanguinity a form of knowing which kind of child one does have; a knowing akin to the one you might have about slaves or animals in which what you know is what you want from them, what they can do for you? You need to know their desire only in so far as it conflicts with your own; there is the knowledge that ownership requires and which makes exploitation, among other things, possible; and then there are the other knowledges, or what might be called 'the unknowledges'. What do you need to know about someone, what do you need to get about them, if ownership is not the issue; knowing as we do, because the play shows us, what happens when ownership is the issue: when knowing is the form ownership takes. Ownership, we might say, involves us in what Žižek called 'the attitude of overinterpretation', something Othello had a lot of, but knew nothing about (paranoia is the attitude of overinterpretation in the service of survival). Sexual jealousy is about trying to get it when you don't get it.

By ownership, in this context, I mean the fantasy of the impossibility of abandonment, of an infallible and unfailing dependence. In this predicament it is not the object but the keeping of the object that is paramount, as though knowing someone was a way of having them in safekeeping. When knowledge of oneself and other people is complicit with such fantasies, it is a form of word-magic. As though it were possible to know oneself and others in a way that would guarantee that one would never be let down. So one paradoxical proposition we might consider is that it is only knowledge of oneself and others that makes betrayal possible. Or, it is the will to knowledge which is the sign of a betrayal that has already happened. What Othello knows, what he thinks he knows, makes what he does possible. At its most minimal we are invited by the play to notice the different kinds of knowing, and where they lead. And we see, most prominently, Othello being seduced into being a certain kind of knowing subject, the one who, like his accomplice, Iago, is supposed to know, supposed by himself. When knowing takes this form it is, as Desdemona discovers, deadly not to know, and deadly to be knowing.

In a passage from *Disowning Knowledge*, which I will be returning to, Stanley Cavell uses Othello to say something about knowledge, torture and dependence. He wants to, as he puts it, cast suspicion on whether we know what it means to know that another exists.

> Nothing could be more certain to Othello than that Desdemona exists; is flesh and blood; is separate from him; other. This is precisely the possibility that tortures him. The content of his torture is the premonition of the existence of another, hence of his own, his own [existence] as dependent and partial . . . His professions of scepticism over her faithfulness are a cover story for a deeper conviction; a terrible doubt covering a yet more terrible certainty, an unstatable certainty . . . this is what I have throughout kept arriving at as the cause of scepticism – the attempt to convert the human condition, the condition of humanity, into an intellectual difficulty, a riddle.

In Cavell's version, Othello uses one certainty to conceal a more disturbing certainty: his supposed knowledge that Desdemona has betrayed him is used to conceal the true conviction that she is a separate person on whom he depends (and is therefore a threat to his self-reliant maleness). What he is really tortured by, Cavell says, is this knowledge of dependence; so, in effect, he has fast-forwarded it to the catastrophe he has always feared – her abandonment – and solved the problem by killing her. And, of course, by murdering her he has indeed ensured that she will never betray him (and she has abandoned him for ever). Tragedy, Cavell writes, 'is the place we are not allowed to escape the consequences, or price, of this cover'. So our cover story is always to deal with, to occlude or obscure, a prior knowledge, that people we depend on we do not and cannot control; when that person was the God of the New Testament, at least after the Reformation, there was no doubt about the other one on whom we depend being beyond our control; once the other one is a person we have no defence.

And yet in Cavell's account here one form of knowing is trumped by another; there is real knowledge, foundational knowledge, one might say – our absolute and intractable dependence on absolutely intractably independent objects – that is hidden by all our other forms of knowing. The cause of scepticism, Cavell writes in a riddling formulation, is 'the attempt to convert the human condition . . . into an intellectual difficulty, a riddle'. If it is a riddle, then if we know enough, if we know the right things in the right way, we can solve it. Whereas the human condition as formulated by Cavell – which is, more or less, the human condition formulated by the psychoanalysis that follows on from Freud – is insoluble. There is nothing we could know about ourselves or another that can solve the problem that other people actually exist, and we are utterly dependent on them as actually existing, separate other people whom we need.

There is nothing to know apart from this, and everything else we know, or claim to know, or are supposed to know, or not know, follows on from this. And mostly, Cavell – and indeed Freud – wants us to note, our knowing, such as it is, is our desperate attempt to conceal this. Scepticism can protect us from this or help us to see it. We have to, in Cavell's language, abrogate the knowing of other people in favour of the acknowledgement of their existence. We mustn't let knowing do the work of acknowledging; otherwise we can end up disbelieving – that is, being unable to prove – the existence of other people and then of ourselves. Knowing other people, in psychoanalytic language, can be a defence, the defence, against acknowledging their actual existence, and what we need their existence for.

What is worth adding to this is that we have to start, developmentally, by knowing ourselves and others – by having, by being allowed, the illusion of such knowledge – in order to make acknowledgement possible. Getting it, at the beginning, is the only way we have of being free to not get it. The illusion of knowing another person creates the possibility, the freedom, of not knowing them; to be free, by not knowing them, to do something else with them. This knowing other people Freud called 'transference', and it was based on, it came from, an earlier illusion of having known the parents, and oneself in relation to the parents. Resolving a transference, then, means not – in the context of a psychoanalytic treatment – releasing the patient from seeing the analyst as though he were someone else (mother, father, siblings, etc.), which means thinking you know who they were, that there was an original knowing; or enabling the patient to displace the transference; it means releasing the patient from the project, which is partly an illusion – a necessary illusion that makes development possible – of knowing and being known (in Cavell's terms, to transform knowledge into acknowledgement). Psychoanalysis, as a treatment, is an opportunity to recover the freedom not to know or be known, and so to find out what people might do together instead. One of its aims, one disclaimed by Freud, was to reseparate sex from knowing.

'I had rather to adopt a child than get it.' The other thing that might be heard in this line – the kind of thing, perhaps, that psychoanalysis encourages – is the idea that, from Brabantio's point of view at this moment in the play, it is better to have children without having sex; that when it comes to having children the sex part should be delegated, as though at this moment something disturbing – something horrifying enough to turn him into a tyrant – has been revealed to him not simply about his daughter and her lover but about sexuality itself. And it might be something like, you can know a daughter but you can't know her sexuality; you can know a person but the one thing you cannot, in any real sense, know is their sexuality; partly because they do not know about it themselves; and partly because it is not the kind of thing that can be known (it isn't information). We can acknowledge that we are desiring creatures, but, in this case, parents might know their children very well but they may know very little about their children's desire, and, of course, vice versa. Only a world that prioritized knowing would need to give such excessive attention to the one thing that cannot be known about a person. Who their children fall in love with shouldn't make too much sense to their parents.

It is extraordinary to Brabantio that his daughter could love a man like Othello; indeed, she seems to him now like an adopted child. He started by knowing her but now he does not (the adopted child being the child with whom the parent does not share the child's entire history, and the child's unknown history is deemed to be decisive: as though a shared history is at least a shared knowledge). Brabantio, through the disclosure of Desdemona's desire, can no longer be the one supposed to know his daughter. What is revealed is the male characters' way of knowing the women, and the consequences of what Melanie Klein called their 'espiste-mophilic instinct'. When it comes to sexuality, we don't get it. But this doesn't mean that we just haven't yet come up with the right way of knowing, the kind of knowing suited to our sexual natures. It means that when it comes to sex we are not going to get it. We may have inklings about it, but we are not going to, as it were, get to the bottom of it. We can know the facts of life, but nothing else. We may, as we say, have sex, but we won't get it.

It seems odd to say that we know people but we don't know them as desiring creatures; that in so far as we can accept people, including the people who are children, as sexual we have to concede that knowing them in any conscious way may not be the best, the most promising, thing we can do with them. We may know what food they like, their favourite colour, their artistic tastes and distastes, and these are things we can know. But it amounts – Freud and Cavell among many other modernist writers suggest – to very little; in fact, what all this knowledge of people discloses is how little knowing can do for us and, indeed, how anguished other people make us; this is presumably acknowledged by the way in which when people fall in love they are so eager to know, and know about each other; as though they are saying to each other in this frenetic passion for intimate knowledge, when it comes to love, knowing doesn't work; when it comes to love, what is revealed is that one desires, but one has no idea what it is that one desires. Or it may be, as Proust wants to persuade us, that this wish to know is more pernicious, less clueless; that what one wants to know about the other, unconsciously, is what will cure us of our desire for them.

Not knowing someone, not getting it, then becomes integral to the project of sustaining desire. The wish to know someone – the wish to get it, the person, the poem, the joke – can be the wish to quell, to temper, anticipatory excitement; or even to get rid of our desire for them. When a man prematurely ejaculates, it is because he knows exactly what a woman is; when a woman takes flight from a man she desires, she is behaving as if she knows what the man is to her. States of conviction are attempts to regulate excitement.

If it were a matter of rational calculation – of the greatest happiness for the greatest number of parts of ourselves – we might just think that we need to work out in which areas of our lives getting it gives us the lives we want, and in which areas not getting it does. And we would probably find that in most areas that matter to us we need, as we say, a bit of both. But if we put the stress on not getting it – or describe what trying to get it precludes us from experiencing – one thing, I think, becomes obvious, though it is slightly absurd; and that is, that all our competence and all our confidence is about getting it. What kind of confidence might we be able to get from not getting it; other, that is, than the kind of confidence that can come from defying, from mocking, the authorities? In the simple reversal, teaching someone how not to ride a bike would either tempt them, paradoxically, just to ride it, or reveal how conformist all the bike riders were. What I am interested in is what might be discovered, or found, or experienced, in the not getting it that might be of value (how, for example, might one write about a poem if one made no attempt to explain it?). Because this, in effect, is what Freud is saying we might do with sexuality; all our inclinations – including parts of the inclination that is psychoanalysis – are to explain it, to know about our desire; to give oneself and others an account. 'What is really a reason for what,' the philosopher Robert Brandom writes in *Reason in Philosophy*, 'depends on how things actually are'; but when it comes to sexuality we never know how things actually are. But in giving an account we make of sexuality, of our desire, something that it is not and can never be. It is as though we are trying to stop it having its effect, prevent it taking its course. This, at least, is one thing Freud suggests, over time, that when it comes to sexuality, we have to give up on knowing, or, rather, since we can't give up on it – that, at least in psychoanalytic terms, where we are traumatized, there we will seek to know and not know, where we are helpless, we will become curious – we have to ironize the knowing that we do about our sexuality (the stories we tell about our sexuality will always be unsettled and unsettling). If we can describe ourselves as not getting it, we are presuming that somebody does; that somebody is presumed or presuming to know. What psychoanalysts mostly know about sex is the strange ineffectuality of so much of their knowledge. What both the

so-called patient and the so-called analyst are so often struck
by in the process of psychoanalysis is how so much of what
seems to be true makes absolutely no predictable difference. Or, more exactly, that the difference that knowing
can make is itself unknowable; that what you can discover
about your own desire, about the history of your desiring,
tells you nothing certain about your future proclivities.

Can we learn how not to know, as well as how to know,
and what could be the benefit that might accrue from this?
Or, in which area of our lives does not knowing, not getting
it, give us more life rather than more deadness? When does
having or wanting to get it narrow our minds? Is there a
taken-for-granted tyranny – is there someone ordering us
around in our minds to try to get it? What psychoanalysis
and literary criticism have in common, at its most minimal,
is the wish to give an account of something, to add on
something of value to what is already there, to redescribe
something with a view to a preferred future. 'Rhetorical
terms,' the literary critic Barbara Johnson writes in *Persons
and Things*, 'aid in the expression of desire; no one seeks
new ways to say what is not desired'. When not getting it
is desired – when we can acknowledge the areas of our
lives in which the wish to get it is a distraction – we might
have the terms for it. It is worth wondering what boundaries those who don't always want to get it will have to
defend. And whether they can get away with it.

On Getting Away with It

Nothing important comes with instructions.

James Richardson, 'Vectors 3.0'

The first use of the phrase 'getting away with it' in Britain – according to the thus far unassailable authority of the *Oxford English Dictionary* – is in Aldous Huxley's novel of 1923, *Antic Hay*. Whether or not this is true – and the margin is only about forty-five years between its first recorded use as American slang and Huxley's novel – it is an unusually revealing place for the phrase to turn up. Isaiah Berlin, in Sybille Bedford's memoir *Aldous Huxley*, explains the power of the early Huxley as a culture-hero for a generation in the following terms: '"the cynical", God-denying Huxley, the object of fear and disapproval . . . the wicked nihilist . . . [the delight of] those young readers who supposed themselves to be indulging in one of the most dangerous and exotic vices of those iconoclastic post-war times'. And Aldous Huxley himself, writing to his father about his immensely successful second novel, described it as, a book written by a member of what I may call the war generation for others of his kind; and . . . it is intended to reflect – fantastically, of course, but none the less faithfully – the life and opinions of an age which has seen the violent disruption of almost all the standards, conventions and values current in the previous epoch.

If the book was intended to reflect 'the life and opinions of an age', and this phrase itself alludes to *The Life and Opinions of Tristram Shandy, Gentleman*, it is because strange disruptions, uncanny discontinuities are in play. The novel in fact opens with the hero Theodore Gumbril's disillusionment about God, and about himself as a schoolteacher; and the story, which is really a series of social encounters with people living the disarray of the times and talking about it, is about Gumbril's forlorn and absurd attempt to go into business; to market his ludicrous invention, the idea for which, he tells his father (another father) '"came . . . like an apocalypse, suddenly, like a divine inspiration. A grand and luminous idea came to me – the idea of Gumbril's Patent Small-Clothes".' 'Small-Clothes' is a euphemism for a new form of underwear, which, he explains, 'may be described as trousers with a pneumatic seat, inflatable by means of a tube fitted with a valve; the whole constructed of stout seamless red rubber, enclosed between two layers of cloth'. This invention, which needless to say comes to nothing, he intends to sell 'to some capitalist, or . . . exploit it commercially myself'. Symbolically, of course, it makes immobility more comfortable, and protects people whose work involves sitting down – from the harder realities. Gumbril takes his invention to a shady entrepreneur called Mr Boldero – almost 'Bold hero', almost 'Bold Eros' – who is enthusiastic about ripping off both Gumbril and the potential purchasers of the product. Huxley introduces him carefully, in what is the most tendentious chapter in the book. Boldero, he writes,

> was always busy, always had twenty different irons in the fire at once, was always fresh, clear-headed, never tired. He was also always unpunctual, always untidy. He had no sense of time or of order. But he got away with it, as he liked to say. He delivered the goods – or rather the good, in the convenient form of cash, delivered themselves, almost miraculously it always seemed to him.

He is opportunistic – 'always had twenty different irons in the fire at once' – and he defies or eludes the usual conventions, he 'had no sense of time or of order'. 'But he got away with it, as he liked to say' – and it is his liking to say it that is important. It is a kind of boast, it has to be announced, and there is pleasure in the saying of it. It is a claim. And the idea of this being akin to a new morality is signalled to us, rather heavy-handedly, by Huxley's shifting the commercial term into the moral term. 'He delivered the goods – or rather the good, in the convenient form of cash'; the other way round would have been crass, but Huxley wants us to see what the Good has become, and what kind of people make it work like this. Boldero is above all explicit, open about how to sell the product. He likes to say that he is exploitative, duplicitous and honest all at once, that these are no longer incompatible.

> 'We want to appeal,' Mr Boldero went on so glibly that Gumbril felt sure he must be quoting somebody else's words, 'to the great instincts and feelings of human-ity . . . They are the sources of action. They spend the money, if I may put it like that.'

' "The modern democratic advertiser," ' he goes on, ' "is entirely above-board. He tells you all about it." ' But he is open and honest in the service of duplicity; he uses science to persuade and mislead; but science can only be used like this, used, that is to say, so convincingly, so plausibly, so unscrupulously, if one knows about literature. ' "There is no better training for modern commerce than a literary education," ' Boldero tells Gumbril. ' "As a practical businessman, I always uphold the ancient universities, especially in their teaching of the Humanities." ' The humanities, a literary education, are a training in getting away with it; in making, in this case, something fatuous into an essential commodity

(' "that's what we can do with our trousers; we can put a message into them, a big, spiritual message" '). Inspired by Boldero, Gumbril begins to recognize his own talents: 'He could have been, he always felt, such a ruthless critic and satirist, such a violent, unscrupulous polemical writer.' Criticism and satire, whether or not they are unscrupulous, are the genres in which people are accused, are shown to be getting away with things when they shouldn't be; in criticism and satire, apparent greatness is exposed and true greatness upheld. But literature, the 'Humanities', are complicit with the new entrepreneurial spirit, with 'modern democratic advertising', being above board, telling you all about it, getting away with it. Literature both helps you get away with it and exposes other people's getting away with it; indeed, it might get away with it by exposing the way other people get away with it. In Boldero's new morality, we don't know what people are doing, we don't know what they are up to, because they are telling us what they are doing; they are above board. And to make matters more complicated, Boldero is a bit like Sterne in *Tristram Shandy*: 'He had no sense of time or of order. But he got away with it, as he liked to say.' Not no sense of time or of order, but a different sense. But he got away with it, as he liked to say.

It is the satirist's and the critic's art not to let people get away with it; but perhaps not letting people get away with things is itself a way of getting away with something else. This is clearly something Huxley is wondering about in *Antic Hay*; what is it like to live in a culture in which the thing people like to say is, 'I got away with it', in which this is a boast? Something you like to say to other people. In which a successful piece of advertising is a picture of moral excellence; in which Gumbril's Patent Small-Clothes are the goods that have become the Good. It would be easy now to say the obvious jeremiad things, or the obvious (capitalist) triumphalism things; to say that a successful 'modern democratic' advertising campaign for Gumbril's Patent Small-Clothes would be an act of moral cynicism or an act of imaginative ingenuity, a triumph of rhetoric over truth and goodness. What are we celebrating when we celebrate people who get away with it? And what are we condemning when we condemn?

The reason that believers don't think of God as 'getting away with it' is that the phrase itself implies the existence of a higher authority. If it means breaking the rules with impunity – eluding the expected consequences, the usual constraints – it also acknowledges that there are rules. It pays tribute to the idea that, in the ordinary way of things, we are under surveillance, that somebody is keeping their eye on us, that we are not masters in our own houses; that we are, in that ambiguous phrase, 'being looked after'. Which is why, as we shall see, getting away with things is among our most confounding experiences. If, as Freud remarks, the child's first successful lie against the parents is his first moment of independence – the moment when he proves to himself that his parents cannot read his mind, and so are not omniscient deities – then it is also the first moment in which he recognizes his abandonment. The privacy of possibility has opened up for him. If you get away with something – though, as we shall also see, it rather depends on what it is – you have done well and you have done badly. You are released but you are also unprotected. You have, at least provisionally, freed yourself from something, but then you have to deal with your new-found freedom. The ambiguity of the phrase is partly to do with the odd picture of freedom it contains. An exhilaration masks a fear.

When you get away with it – let's call the 'it', for the sake of argument, a crime, even though 'getting away with it' can change its status – something about the higher authority has been exposed; its weakness, its fallibility, its capacity for oversight, certainly its omnipotence; and so something about your relationship to this authority has changed – you have, for example, been able to enact your challenge to it; you have gone from taking it for granted to testing its reach. What has been recovered, or discovered, is not, in actuality, your freedom, at least not yet, but your release, for however long. This interim, this uncertain threshold, is obviously vital in the total process. When do you know that you have got away with it? And what do you think of as providing evidence? Clearly, if you are living on the run you have not got away with it, you are still trying to. What do you do in, or with, that period of release? How, if at all, does it change your description of the powers you have, for the time being, slipped? Think of the child who has told his first successful lie; he is living in the same country now, but it is another country as well. What, after all, if anything, will the powers that be do once they notice what has happened? Their not doing anything, apparently, might make them seem more powerful. My successful crime may just reveal how unfathomable their authority really is.

When we are talking about getting away with something we are talking about the dizzying possibility of not being punished for getting what we think we want (what Sartre called 'the vertigo of freedom'; freedom, for this short man, was to do with heights). And since it is the whole idea of punishment that makes so many of our narratives hang together – the popular end that gives us a beginning and a middle, which are not always easy to find – getting away with something also means rewriting the story. If you do get away with something, you have revised your expectations, narrative expectations included. Most stories – and all morally improving stories – are about why and how we can't get away with the things we shouldn't be getting away with; they are about why, to adapt Stanley Fish's title, there's no such thing as getting away with it, and it's a good thing too. Most stories, that is to say, confirm the (constitutive) idea of transgression. They are about why we can't and don't get away with things, or about why we don't really want to – why we are such bad liars – which often amounts to the same thing (imagine what would have happened to Oedipus, not to mention psychoanalysis, if he had got away with it, if he had lived quite happily ever after). If it is the possibility, the anticipation, of getting away with something that is among our greatest excitements, then the unlikelihood of such things happening is the complementary reassurance. 'Daydream' – the wishful fantasies of everyday life – is our word for getting away with it; reality tends to be the place invoked for where this may not be possible.

But as a preliminary we need to work out how we picture what the phrase describes, and this involves working out what the 'it' is. At its most literal, if you get away with something you take it with you; you've probably stolen it, but you could have got away with asking for it, or just hinting that you coveted it. It must, though, feel like a theft; the 'it' must belong to someone else. Indeed, it might be one of the ways you would know what belonged to whom; if you got away with it, it didn't, until then, in any sense belong to you. We picture somebody taking something away, probably an object, and not wanting to return it. And yet, of course, what the phrase conveys above all is getting away with not being punished; what you get away with is the object of desire and no penalty; that's what the 'it' is, two 'its'. The object may never be recovered – may, in some sense, still be in my safekeeping – but only if I am caught and punished will I have failed to get away with it. The stolen object makes the punishment possible; but only the absence of punishment means that I really got away with it. Getting away with it is about what might be called the built-in consequences of wanting things, though the consequences can really be said to be built in only if no one ever gets away with it. Getting away with it is a new species of prediction; it predicts unpredictable, literally unknowable, consequences for getting what we want when it doesn't belong to us. If you take something that doesn't belong to you, and you get away with it, you will have to work out what you can do with it. Rules don't make sense if it is impossible to break them, and rules are only rules if there are penalties for breaking them. Getting away with things, as both wish and accomplishment, doesn't sound like news that stays news.

Like many things that seem perennial – we can't imagine a time when people didn't want to get away with things – the phrase 'getting away with it' is anything but, as we shall see. It locates itself in time and space with unusual clarity. And this, in itself, might give us pause. *Chambers Twentieth Century Dictionary* has: 'get away with (something), to pull something off: to carry a thing through successfully or with impunity'. Even the definition has its own necessary ambiguity, 'to pull something off' is at once an exposure and a success; and with its own telling qualification, 'successfully *or* with impunity'; not necessarily the same thing. *Collins English Dictionary* prefers the unequivocally illicit implication: 'get away with. 1. to steal and escape (with money, goods, etc.); 2. to do (something wrong, illegal, etc.) without being discovered or punished, or with only a minor punishment'. What the *Collins* definition gives us is that getting away with something is not merely to do with wrongdoing, it is itself wrongdoing; it involves taking something that was not yours, and so can't be yours. As if you can get away with it only if the 'it' is some kind of crime; you know you have committed a crime when, however briefly, you think of yourself as having got away with something. The difference between being discovered *or* punished is noteworthy – echoing *Chambers* 'to carry a thing through successfully *or* with impunity' – suggesting as it does the morality of the-only-crime-is-to-get-caught. The link both definitions make is between succeeding at something and the illicit, and succeeding at the illicit, of which presumably lying, the successful lie, is our most familiar example. But what we are alerted to here is that I might get away with writing a Petrarchan sonnet, I might carry it off successfully; I might get away with plagiarism because my borrowing is undiscovered. There are, in other words, important links between doing something well and doing it with impunity. If I am not punished by critics, I know my sonnet is a success. Not being punished can be a sign of success in actions that we had not thought of as illicit. For something to be done with impunity, for something to go unpunished, can be a bad thing and a good thing, and it can be both, depending upon one's point of view.

But, clearly, getting away with something, doing it with impunity, leads us to the idea of being found out; because we have only ever got away with something until we are found out. And yet, of course, we have always already been found out by ourselves. Getting away with it is also, then, a way of talking about the relationship between the inside and the outside, between our own privacy and what goes on between ourselves and other people. Our acts can be undiscovered by others only if we have first noticed them ourselves. But our acts do not necessarily go unpunished if they are noticed only by ourselves. 'Conscience does make cowards of us all' because we see ourselves acting. What we call the mind tends to be the place where we get away with things –

we call this, as I said, daydream, erotic fantasy, wish-fulfilment; and the mind, at least in the Freudian story, is also the place where, as Hamlet remarks, no one ever gets away with anything. What Lacan calls 'the obscene super-ego' is far more scrupulous in its attentions, and more brutal in its punishments, than external authority can ever be. One of the reassurances of psychoanalysis is that it shows us that we can't get away with anything, even our thoughts; 'guilt' is our word for not getting away with it. Getting away with it, in the fullest sense, would mean not feeling guilty, an exorbitant wish we will have to come back to.

No one in *Hamlet* gets away with anything; indeed, that's what tragedies are, dramas in which people, in the most extreme ways possible, don't get away with things. But the other sense in which no one in *Hamlet*, indeed, no one in Shakespeare, gets away with anything is that the phrase did not, in our sense of it, exist in the early seventeenth century. It is, as I said, a phrase that can be located accurately, though it is perhaps surprising to find out that its provenance is as American slang, and it was used in America from the late nineteenth century, the first citation being 1878. The definition in the *OED* is:

to get away with (US slang), to get the better of, to beat in a contest. Also (colloq., orig. US) to carry off successfully; to succeed in winning or stealing; to do (something) with impunity; frequently in phrase, to get away with it, to succeed in what one tries; to act without being detected or punished; so, to get away with murder: to get away with anything; to do whatever one wishes.

In its early usage, as American slang, perhaps unsurprisingly given the times and the economic ethos, it's almost exclusively about success – about the successfully completed action – and it covers 'winning or stealing'. And it also, interestingly, includes the idea of winning a contest, as though in any successful competition there may be a degree of getting away with something, that the agonistic is not immune from luck or duplicity.

There is certainly a kind of triumphalism, a beating of the system, a getting-ahead in whatever way possible, which the slang seems to promote: good things, necessary things, impressive things, it seems to say, may involve breaking the rules; that the ends don't merely justify the means, they can celebrate them. That there may even be something noble or glorious or heroic in getting away with something; indeed, the phrase might announce a new version of heroism. The hero is not the person who plays by the rules but the person who doesn't; that courage means whatever you have to do to win; that the honourable thing could be to do what you wish; and the only thing that matters about a wish is that you are successful in realizing it. Morality in this entrepreneurial pragmatism could be of any use only if it was in the service of success. The definition in the *OED* is like an advertisement for success, a wake-up call for all the good people who run the risk, in this particular world, of being losers (in US slang of approximately the same time, a 'loser' was, according to the *OED*, 'a convicted criminal'). In a morally paradoxical move it is as though, in the slang phrase 'getting away with it', criminality, the disregarding of the rules for personal gain, was being normalized.

The definition makes an implicit link – in the way only dictionaries can, which makes them such provocative reading matter – between success and not being punished for what one does, as though punishment was the contrary, the obverse, of success: 'to succeed in what one tries; to act without being detected or punished'. In what sense does success – the successful crime as much as the successful work of art – depend upon not being detected or punished? One of the American *Webster's* definitions is 'to accomplish with impunity; avoid punishment', as though the successful crime, like the successful work of art, is itself defined by the ways in which it has managed to avoid punishment. To accomplish things with impunity is success. And we do, after all, punish works of art that are not successful; and we call this punishment, in the case of literature, literary criticism.

If the question one can usefully ask of any work of philosophy is, what are the arguments the philosopher believes people must not be allowed to get away with, in literary studies it is clearly not only the so-called arguments that are being assessed; but there are still things the critic believes that the writer should not be allowed to get away with. And there is always some catastrophe that the philosopher or critic believes will ensue if the writer in question is allowed to get away with it (it would be useful if we could be given a picture of what the world would look like after the catastrophe, but this rarely happens). So when the American philosopher John Searle, in his book *Freedom and Neurobiology*, reports back in the aftermath, as it were, it is worth taking note. 'One of the most stunning cultural developments of the past few centuries,' he writes,

> was the rise of the nation-state as the ultimate focus of collective loyalty in a society. People have, for example, been willing to fight and die for the United States or Germany or France or Japan in a way that they would not be willing to fight and die for Kansas City or Vitry-le-François.
>
> How do governments, so to speak, get away with it? That is, how does the government manage as a system of status function superior to other status functions?

One of the keys, perhaps the most important key, is that typically governments have a monopoly on organised violence. Furthermore, because they have a monopoly on the police and the armed forces, they in effect have control of a territory in a way that corporations, churches and ski clubs do not control a territory. The combination of control of the land plus a monopoly on organised violence guarantees government the ultimate power role within competing systems of status functions . . . Though military and police power are different from political power, there is no such thing as government, no such thing as political power, without police power and military power.

Governments are described by Searle as getting away with this – getting people to die for their nation-state – through 'a monopoly on organised violence'. The phrase acknowledges they have been wholly successful, but implies that there was a higher authority that they defeated; that there was something unscrupulous about the ways these modern governments forged an ultimate focus of collective loyalty. Searle is saying, if you do X, this is what happens; if people get away with something – and he noticeably doesn't quite say what it is – this is the aftermath. When someone, in this case modern governments, get away with something, it is not inevitable that they should. If the nation-state can manage only through violence, then something has been violated – call it freedom of thought and speech – but who can punish them? Or what would they feel punished by? Those who get away with things change the taste by which they can be judged. Searle asks 'How do governments . . . get away with it?' as if they haven't yet done so or as if something more powerful could stop them; indeed, he implies either that there is something more powerful than 'a monopoly on or-ganised violence', or that some other group should have this monopoly and use it for other ends. It sounds like a secular version of what was once a theological question: what would it be to punish the person, so to speak, who has all the power? And the answer would be that you would have to be the kind of person who changed the criteria of judgement; you can accuse someone of getting away with something only if you know what the rules are. If you believe that the focus of collective loyalty in a society should be the nation-state, then anyone who puts Church above country is a traitor and shouldn't get away with it.

But what if getting away with it became the rule? If we can't get away with it because there are higher authorities, but the highest authorities can, in the words of the *OED*, 'do (something) with impunity' (in the words of *Webster's*, 'avoid punishment'), then they are not the ones who are getting away with anything; they are the ones who have got away. You will use the phrase 'getting away with it' only when a higher authority is appealed to. So if getting away with it were to become, as the American slang intimated – such as Searle's example rather suggests – the new ethos, the thing to do, then quite quickly there would be no such thing as getting away with it. If God is dead, it is not that everything is permitted – which would simply be his reappearance as the permitter rather than the forbidder – but that there will be no more getting away with it. I think it is worth wondering, if we can imagine such a thing, what kind of loss that might be.

We have to imagine a very paradoxical thing: not that there are no rules – indeed, the opposite, that there are rules we are very impressed by – but our project, our new moral law, so to speak, is to get away with breaking them; the new question being, as Searle suggests, not why did they get away with it, but how? We might have to take seriously the possibility, intimated by the definitions of the phrase in the *OED* and *Webster's*, that a new morality was being announced towards the end of the nineteenth century in America. In this new morality it is not that rules are made to be broken, but that rules are made to be broken without being punished for doing so. We publicly consent to rules that privately we seek to outwit. And it is only because the rules matter to us so much that our satisfaction is in avoiding being punished for breaking them. In this apotheosis of privacy we have it both ways: we believe in higher authorities and we believe in avoiding punishment. In the beginning the idea was that, at least in a democracy, once you had consented to the laws, you tried to abide by them; then the idea was that once you had consented to the rules, you tried to break them without being caught, which left the rules in place and promised you the things you wanted. In the world of getting-away-with-it, your desire is not that the rules be changed – indeed, if your pleasure is in getting away with it, you depend upon the rules – but that you find out how not to be constrained by them. It is only if you want to put a stop to getting away with something that you change the rules. No one gets away with being patriotic now, with being loyal to the nation-state. The new morality of getting-away-with-it, it is worth noting, is a world apparently without guilt; a world in which there are no internalized authorities, no conscience, only external authorities to avoid being punished by.

Since getting away with it is rule-bound, it is possible in virtually all our rule-bound activities. I say 'virtually all' because no one can exempt themselves from or cheat, by definition, the rules of an omnipotent deity or the laws of nature. No one is going to get away with not breathing for three weeks, or defying the rules of gravity; these are the rules one cannot even try to get away with breaking. You can get away with it only if the rule is, as we say, man-made. Indeed, this might be a good way of distinguishing between rules one can get away with breaking and those which one can't (it is hubris or arrogance or madness when you try to find out which is which). Clearly, aesthetic rules can be broken, rules of form and genre; and in retrospect many innovations in the arts seem to come about precisely as a result of rules being broken. Whereas the only way in which a successful criminal tends to change the law is by causing it to be tightened. If getting away with it is avoiding the official, the accepted, consequences of your desire, then we should also note the consequences of people's having got away with things. Realms of practice can be distinguished by what they end up calling those people who get away with breaking the rules.

One of the things I want to consider – indeed, one of the things that is integral to the subject – is a simple fact: that getting away with things, whatever else it is, is always a pleasure, however brief. We like to do it ourselves, and we like to hear of other people who do it. At its most minimal, getting away with something – not paying on the train, cheating successfully in an exam, insider dealing – can be thrilling. We are impressed even when we are appalled (Searle described 'the rise of the nation-state as the ultimate focus of collective loyalty' as

'One of the most stunning cultural developments of the past few centuries'). I want to suggest that it is only in the arts that we can be open about the pleasures of getting away with it; that it is in the arts that getting away with it can be publicly discussed in all its complexity. In politics, as in business, it has to be at least publicly condemned, however gleefully enjoyed it is in private. When we admire people for breaking a law that we have consented to, we put ourselves in a difficult position. It is this position that the arts are particularly well suited to explore.

If getting away with it is always an acknowledgement of higher authorities – indeed, brings them into focus, unlike virtually anything else, because they are at once strangely absent and powerfully present in their absence – then accounts both of and by people getting away with things are going to be stories about submission, whatever else they are stories about. So I want to begin with a story about literary criticism, a story about the critics' submission, or otherwise, to literature. Geoffrey Hartman has been an eloquent critic of this view, suggesting that one of the ways we idealize literature is to disparage the critic. There are things that the critic won't let the writer get away with; but the critic, who is also a writer, must not be allowed to get away with positioning himself as a higher authority than the writer herself. 'The English tradition in criticism,' he writes in *Criticism in the Wilderness*,

> is sublimated chatter; but it is also animated by its fierce ability to draw reputation into question. Even Shakespeare had once to be made safe; and Milton is restored, after Leavis, to his bad eminence. This power to alter reputations is formidable, and it shows that criticism has an unacknowledged penchant for reversal in it, which is near daemonic, and which brings it close to the primacy of art. This penchant, of course, can be dismissed as the sin of envy: as a drive for primacy, like Satan's or Iago's. Yet, Lukács remarked, there is something ironic about the critic's subordination of himself to the work reviewed. At best he keeps testing that work, that apparent greatness, and by force of doubt or enthusiasm puts it more patently before us. He plays the role now of accuser, now of God . . . But [criticism] can also frighten us by opening a breach – or the possibility of transvaluation – in almost every received value.

There is the 'apparent greatness' of the work, and the apparent greatness of God and Christ to Satan in *Paradise Lost*, and of Othello and Cassio to Iago (and in the allusion to Nietzsche's 'transvaluation of all values' a suggestion of just how easily greatness can become apparent greatness from a different point of view). The 'apparent greatness' of the work can be redescribed by the critic as getting away with a greatness that may not be deserved, or is, at the very least, subject to question. The implication here is that getting away with something that the text might seem to have carried off, to have succeeded in, is a pretence, a sham; and that there is a way of describing it that will expose this. What this requires, though, and Hartman places the critic here, is that someone sets himself up as a competing authority. 'Criticism,' Hartman writes, 'has an unacknowledged penchant for reversal in it, which is near daemonic, and which brings it close to the primacy of art.' 'Reversal' here means that the omnipotent figure previously referred to as God can be accused of getting away with something; that a world in which people can accuse each other of getting away with things is a world of competing authority, a world in which there is no final or absolute authority. A world, as Hartman puts it, of 'daemonic' reversals. The critic, by making the case for only the apparent greatness of the work, is becoming a potential rival. At their best, critics show what writers are getting away with, in both senses – what they are successfully achieving, whatever the means, and how they are cheating us.

Hartman's position vis-à-vis the critic is not worlds apart from the philosopher Richard Rorty's 'pragmatist way', though Hartman himself would not, I imagine, want to describe it like this. 'If we do things the pragma-tist way,' Rorty writes in *What's the Use of Truth* (co-author Pascal Engel),

we will no longer think of ourselves as having responsibilities towards non-human entities such as truth or
reality. I have often suggested that we regard pragmatism
as an attempt to complete the project common to the
Renaissance humanists and the Enlightenment. The pragmatists think that it is time to stop believing that we have
obligations to God or to some God surrogate. The pragmatism of James, like the existentialism of Sartre, is an
attempt to convince us to stop inventing such surrogates.

To try to get away with something is to try to replace one
set of obligations with another. What Hartman and Rorty
are speaking up for is a world in which greatness can be
redescribed as apparent greatness, in which all greatness
can be accused of trying to get away with something (the
claim of greatness, of priority). When we ask of a writer,
what is she trying to get away with, we are asking both
what authority does she feel answerable to, and what
new set of obligations is she trying to meet or create? If
we 'no longer think of ourselves as having responsibilities
towards non-human entities such as truth or reality',
we are fairly and squarely in the world of getting away
with it. If there is no absolute authority, no such thing as
omnipotence or omniscience, we are free to redescribe
all forms of authority, as John Searle described modern
governments, as simply powerful ways of getting away
with something. There is trying to get away with it, the
means; there is letting people get away with it, colluding

with the means; and there is trying to stop people getting away with it, the corrections.

Stopping people getting away with something, it should be noted, is the restoration of prior authority. It is conservative. But getting away with it is also conservative of the status quo in so far as it is not an attempt to change the law but to elude it. To find where it is vulnerable, and to keep it in place. To triumph over it in secret; to sustain the pleasure of breaking the law and not breaking it at the same time. In what sense, after all, have I broken the law if no one knows I have done it? Or if the appropriate people – the authorities – never find out? Getting away with it is like an apparently private language within and made possible by a public language; like a dialect. It is as though the law has let me break the law, as long as I (we) keep it secret; the law is complicit with my breaking it by not being omnipotent. Or, to put it another way, when I get away with it, when I get away with breaking the law, I change but the law doesn't. I have found my loophole. Greatness has become apparent greatness.

Towards the end of the nineteenth century in America, as I've said, 'getting away with it' was a new thing that people could say that they could do. As slang – 'the special vocabulary used by any set of persons of a low or disreputable character', as the *OED* quaintly puts it – it was itself something people, low and disreputable ones, were getting away with saying. It is, of course, no longer slang, and no longer just American; it has been seamlessly assimilated, and we can't imagine life without it. Or life, modern life, has made it necessary. So I want to wonder, by way of conclusion: What has been added to the moral life by this phrase? What has it added to the stock of available reality? There is, after all, a long and venerable tradition of duplicity, of lying, cheating, hypocrisy, double standards; the law and its breaking are not news. No one is described as 'getting away with it', or anything, in *Othello*, *Paradise Lost* or *Mansfield Park*; no one in Dickens, or even Henry James, the concordances tell us, are 'getting away with it'; though we might say, sensibly, that they are doing the equivalent, but without finding or needing our modern phrase for it. So much of what we call literature is about people getting away with things, or not, but until the late nineteenth century they just didn't put it like this. They were doing it, but they didn't have this precise phrase for it; a phrase that publicizes something that, in order to work, has to be kept secret. Announcing that I got away with it – giving a lecture that was written by someone else – could be the beginning of the end. Getting away with it – as a talent, as a skill – is something you would keep to yourself, or only tell people who were on your side; indeed, the telling of it would create a group. But what if getting away with it was a new moral principle or project? What if it announced a new morality? In this new morality – which sounds like a moral game, or a parody of the idea of morality – moral excellence would reside in being able to successfully exempt yourself from rules you have consented to. You would always be getting out of it – the law you promote and claim to abide by. The Good Person would be replaced by the Impressive Person; and what would impress would be the breaking of rules without punishment; the bearable lightness of being. Where once there were the principled, now there would be the opportunists; the clever would displace the pious.

These new moralists would not be amoral, because they would depend on the law for their new morality. They would be self-confessed double agents. They would be able to practise their duplicity only by advertising it. Being caught would be the crime. They would need to keep the world as it is, not to go on rebelling against it, but to go on cheating it. They would be pro law and order. And they would have only one real enemy: a law that was infallible, or, to put it another way, an authority that was omniscient. They would be the lovers of loopholes, of apparent greatness, of things one can find a way round. From one point of view, one might say, it would be a morality for the disillusioned; or, rather, for those who want to believe in higher authorities, and don't want to believe in them, *at the same time*.

On Getting Out of It

To unlock the innermost secret of morality and culture
is to know simply: what to avoid.

Philip Rieff, *Charisma*

Philip Larkin told John Haffenden (in *Poets in
Conversation*) that he took 'great care' in ordering the
poems in a collection. 'I treat them,' he said, 'like a
music-hall bill: you know, contrast, difference in length,
the comic, the Irish tenor, bring on the girls.' Larkin,
like many of the best interviewees, gets into the question by getting out of it; Haffenden's studious question
'Do you take great care in ordering the poems in a
collection?' is taken up by Larkin with requisite bathos:
'Yes, great care. I treat them like a music-hall bill.' The
care is taken to keep the reader entertained, to hold her
attention; the writer is up against the reader's distract-
edness, her failing concentration. The wish always to
be somewhere else, at least in one's mind. The get-out
clause in any act of reading.

Larkin was a poet acutely aware of the Importance of
Elsewhere, of what happens, as he writes in the poem of

that title, when 'no elsewhere underwrites my existence'. And a surprisingly large number of his poems are about, one way or another, that most fundamental experience of elsewhere: leaving home. Leavings, and the anticipations of departure, are everywhere in Larkin's writing. But in this Poetry of Departures one poem stands out, perhaps his most famous and certainly the most notorious, for the starkness of its directive. Placed carefully between 'Homage to a Government', a poem about the withdrawal of British troops from Aden, and 'How Distant', a poem about 'the departure of young men / ... keen / 'Simply to get away', there is that poem called 'This Be the Verse'; a haunting verse with a line that Larkin feared he may not be able to get away from (or with). ('I was wondering,' he said in an interview for the *Observer*, 'whether in the *New Oxford Dictionary of Quotations* I was going to be lumbered with "They fuck you up, your mum and dad". I had it on good authority that this is what they had been told is my best-known line, and I wouldn't want it thought that I didn't like my parents.') This verse from a secular bible begins with an allusion to those people always referred to in a winning phrase as 'our first parents':

They fuck you up, your mum and dad.
They may not mean to, but they do.
They fill you with the faults they had

And add some extra, just for you.
But they were fucked up in their turn
By fools in old-style hats and coats,
Who half the time were soppy-stern
And half at one another's throats.

Man hands on misery to man.
It deepens like a coastal shelf.
Get out as early as you can,
And don't have any kids yourself.

Larkin first mentions this poem in a letter to Anthony
Thwaite of 1971: 'Talking of poetry, I've dashed off a
little piece suitable for Ann's next *Garden of Verses.*'
Thwaite's wife, Ann, edited an annual of new writing
for children called *Allsorts*. As new writing for children
goes, this seems just the job. But as new writing for
adults, it is in some ways a more enigmatic poem than
it claims it wants to be. It is a protest poem with a
very clear message, and therefore an unusual poem
for Larkin, who always fights shy of writing didactic
poems, and tends to ironize the voicing of unequivocal
positions. It is the nuances of the utterly opinionated
that his poems tend to, and indeed that make him such
a riveting interviewee. And 'This Be the Verse', of
course, has echoes and suggestions; it can be read as a
poem about poetic inheritance; there is an intimation,

as there often is in his poetry, of a full-blown, barely contained romanticism, those who the gods favour die young (and childless). And there is Larkin's abiding preoccupation in the poem about not having children (not having children, of course, ensures that they will never leave home). And there are the fleeting and subtle ambiguities that Larkin never wants, and never wants us, to make a literary critical meal of. Your mum and dad 'fuck you up' but they also fuck you into being. 'They fill you with the faults they had / And add some extra, just for you' implies that it could be 'just for you' in both senses; and that there is poetic justice in the pun on 'just', at least in this context.

But though the poem insists on the inevitabilities it portrays – on the helpless and hopeless determinisms that our lives are heir to – it ends with a flourish; it ends, as though coming from nowhere, with the possibility of freedom; as though existentialism is stronger than geology; as though leaving home and not having children was virtually redemptive; as though 'This Be the Verse' is 'What Is to Be Done?'; 'Get out as early as you can, / And don't have any kids yourself.' Leave home and the family as soon as possible, and don't have another one. It's not quite Christ to the disciples because the only thing that is affirmed is the getting out. The project, so to speak, is to stop the relentless transmission of misery. What is believed in, or at least what is being proffered and proposed, is simply the getting out, the breaking of the cycle.

And yet, to echo Isaiah Berlin's distinction between freedom from and for, there is the question raised in this poem of the difference between getting out from and getting out for; and it raises this question in a very provocative way. What do you do after you get out? Once the family and the having of children, once home and reproduction have been avoided or repudiated, what is a life for? And especially if 'they' have already fucked you up, what is getting out going to do for you since the terrible thing has already happened? You might say, I suppose, that the narrator of the poem is telling us to be the guardians or protectors of all the unconceived children; that it would be good, for us and for them, for us not to inflict life on them ('I've said that depression is to me as daffodils were to Wordsworth,' Larkin remarked to Haffenden, which would make depression restorative as a form of memory). And the end of the poem is half banal – most of us would probably agree that it's probably better to leave home as soon as possible, and half 'soppy-stern' and at our throats about not having children. The get-out proposed, and it is artfully staged, leaves us wondering whether it may be unduly omniscient. It is one thing to be sceptical of post-Enlightenment myths of progress; it is another thing to start (prophetically) predicting the future. Myths of decline are myths of progress inverted.

Human unhappiness is not obviously subject to the same laws as coastal shelves, and coastal shelves don't deepen with the kind of inevitability Larkin wants from them. The myth of the Fall is replaced with an erosion – or corrosion – myth; what was once called original sin, the fault of our first parents who also didn't mean it, has become the universal acid. It can be contained only by opting out. This is what we get out for: to break the natural order (as though we could). Larkin, one might say, always knew what he didn't want, but this knowledge only made him sceptical of what he thought he did want. He wanted a life untramelled by family life.

I want to use Larkin's remarkable poem as a pretext for saying that getting out of things is all too easily a form of spurious omniscience. It is as though when we get out of something we know too much: we act as if we know far more than we could – about what would happen if we stayed. That in order to free ourselves from certain things we have to fake an omniscience about the future; and acknowledging this need not be a (masochistic) counsel to endure oppression, but another way of thinking out alternatives. Sometimes, perhaps more often than we realize, we live as if we know more about the experiences we don't have than about the experiences we do have. And sometimes we need to be able to do this in order to free ourselves. The conviction of Larkin's narrator comes from his certainty of what will happen to us if we have children. But of course the one thing you cannot know about having children is what it is like to have children if you haven't got them. Perhaps the narrator of Larkin's poem has had children and is speaking from bitter experience. But by 1971 Larkin's readers mostly knew that Larkin didn't have children himself, and probably imagined that they had a good idea of what Larkin thought of children – or 'nippers', as he calls them in 'Self's the Man' – and family life. Usually the omniscience about what one is getting out from colours one's sense of what one is getting out for. Unusually, 'This Be the Verse' does not offer us the usual consolation of a preferred object. Knowing what you don't want doesn't mean knowing what you do want. This be the verse.

The risk, in a way, is that the omniscience about what one is getting out of – a relationship, a commitment, an arrangement – is matched by an omniscience about what one is getting out for. In the simple pleasure-pain calculus, one is poised between the unsatisfying object from which one must be freed and the preferred, potentially satisfying object that one seeks. The so-called knowledge one has of what will happen if one doesn't get out is the albeit paradoxical knowledge of an uncompleted action.

When someone wants a get-out clause in a contract, or indeed in a relationship, they are allowing for the possibility that something better might turn up; they know that there might be something better, which they need to include in their calculations. Needing to formalize this possibility acknowledges, at its most minimal, that I may not have got what I most want, even if I don't know what that is. And there is, of course, an optimism in assuming that better things may be coming down the line. If get-out clauses lack commitment, they also underwrite an open-ness about the future. My get-out clause, contracted publicly or reassuringly affirmed in the apparent privacy of my own mind, is my uncertainty about my own desire. Only God, presumably, has no need of such things.

And yet, in the poetry of conjunctions that dictionary definitions provide, the phrase 'get out', when it is not the starkest of imperatives, is unusually suggestive. *Chambers Twentieth Century Dictionary* has 'to produce: to extricate oneself'; which is itself reminiscent of Sartre's remark apropos of Genet that 'genius' is the word we use for people who get themselves out of impossible situations. It may be that to produce something is to extricate oneself from something. It also means, as *Collins English Dictionary* tells us, 'to make or become known; publish or be published; 3. to express with difficulty; 4. to extract (information or money) . . . to get a confes-sion out of a criminal; 5. to gain or receive something, esp. something of significance or value: you get out of life what you put into it'. Or, equally plausible, you put into life what you get out of it. Getting out, in its various senses, refers to articulation and its difficulties; and to releases, evasions and avoidances. To get out of something may be a blessed relief, but it may also be an unfathomable loss: 'You can withdraw from the sufferings of the world – that possibility is open to you and accords with your nature – but perhaps that withdrawal is the only suffering you might be able to avoid,' Kafka wrote in his notebook, *Zürau Aphorisms*. Getting out, the possibility that is open to us and that might accord with our nature – and what psychoanalysis was later to call 'the mechanisms of defence' as a way of stressing just how automatic our avoidances are, like a machine in the organism – is always a missing-out, whatever else it is. The exhilarations of release cannot always counter the losses incurred. It is worth wondering what we have had to dispense with in order to look forward.

So I want to propose two things, one a supposition and one a definition. My supposition is that sometimes – perhaps more often than not – we think we know more about the experiences we don't have than about the experiences that we do have, 'frustration' being our word for the experience of not having an experience. I am struck, for example, by how much people talk in psychoanalytic treatment about the experiences they have not had in the experiences that they have had; and how authoritatively, with what passion and conviction, they talk about what they have missed out on. It is not unusual, say, for each member of a couple to know exactly what is missing in their partner; and to know, by the same token, how their lives would be different, that is, so much better, if their partner would change in particular ways. This is my supposition: we live as if we know more about the experiences we haven't had than about the experiences we have had. And certain ways of reading aid and abet this strange form of authority – the authority of inexperience, the conviction we gain from not having done things (after reading D. H. Lawrence as an adolescent I knew no one who knew more about the relations between men and women than myself).

I remember a child telling me in a session – a child who believed, as many children do, that being an adult is the solution to being a child – that the reason he wanted to be bigger was because he wouldn't have to want to be bigger. I take it that wanting to be older for a child is wanting to have the experiences that can only be looked forward to; and I take it that the allure, the power of reading experiences in childhood and adolescence is that they prefigure what might be possible. They are essentially about the experiences the child and the adolescent haven't had. 'Perhaps it is only in childhood,' Graham Greene writes in his essay 'The Lost Child',

> that books have any deep influence on our lives. In later life we admire, we are entertained, we may modify some

views we already hold, but we are more likely to find in books merely a confirmation of what is in our minds already . . .

But in childhood all books are books of divination, telling us about the future, and like the fortune-teller who sees a long journey in the cards or death by water they influence the future. I suppose that is why books excited us so much.

The desire in childhood reading, Greene tells us, is for experiences we haven't yet had; as children we are not just lacking these experiences, we are not yet ready for them; because they are what we want, they are what we want to know about. What the child divines in the book is what he may be capable of; childhood is the developing of an appetite for future possibility. We know more about the experiences we don't have than about the experiences we do have. Though it is, as we shall see, a strange kind of knowing; and it goes back a long way. When Freud wanted to persuade us that perception was distorted by wish, he wanted to persuade us that we tend to see merely what we want in what is there, and that knowing (and not-knowing) is all to do with wanting rather than with truth. We see a future of satisfaction in a present of deprivation. When we look forward, as we can't help but do, something in the present moment is always being overridden.

If 'frustration' is the word we use for the experience of not having an experience we want, that peculiarly insistent form of knowledge called the 'knowledge of deprivation', then childhood reading in Greene's terms answers to this deprivation. For children who love reading it meets a need; it gives them a picture, a drama, of what is possible, which becomes what they want. But by the same token, Greene's description of adult reading – 'In later life we admire, we are entertained, we may modify some views we already hold, but we are more likely to find in books merely a confirmation of what is in our minds already' – is all about the aspiration to stay the same. 'As in a love affair,' Greene adds, 'it is our own features that we see reflected flatteringly back.' Like people who come for psychotherapy, who want to change by remaining the same, the adult reader, in Greene's view, is working hard at keeping the future like the past. The child, like Greene himself, is a traveller; the adult has arrived: the narcissism of anticipation is replaced by the narcissism of settlement. The child wants to be reassured that there is an enlivening future; the adult wants to be reassured that there isn't. The child's desire is to get out of childhood, the adult's desire is to get out of wanting to change.

To have our own features 'reflected flatteringly back' is the essentially narcissistic project in what Freud calls 'repression', the burying in oneself of what one prefers not to know or feel, and which Clara Thompson, in an illuminating parenthesis in *Psychoanalysis, Evolution and Developments*, defines as 'making an experience unconscious' (and she defines 'resistance' as 'the way in which it is kept unconscious'). In other words, repression means that the experience – or an experience – is being had somewhere in the individual, but not in the conscious subject. (Greene's adult reader may be simply working harder, if he is a keen reader, to render his experiences unconscious.) So if my supposition is that we live as if we know more about the experiences that we don't have than about the experiences that we do have, and that this can be a way of avoiding desired experiences, the knowledge of frustration becoming a refuge, a sulk, a grudge, an addictive grievance; then my definition is that what Freud calls 'repression' is a way of getting into something by getting out of it (the neurotic keeps arriving at the place he is trying to escape from; he can get to his destination only by trying to avoid it). Repression is what we do with the experiences that we cannot let ourselves have. We set them aside so as not to be troubled by them again.

The philosopher Richard Boothby has a useful summary of Freud's story about repression, about the how and the why of the ego in its attempt to get out of certain experiences. It is, Boothby writes in *Sex on the Couch*,

Freud's assumption that we are animated by a great heterogeneity of impulses. We are, at some basic level of ourselves, a chaos of conflicting urges. Ego thus refers to the restricted economy of impulses that grounds my feeling of having a stable and predictable identity. The ego selects from a range of impulse energies and leaves the others behind. 'Id' names the remainder of my urges and incipient acts that have been excluded from the ego and held in repression.

Graham Greene's adult reader who wants to 'find in books merely a confirmation' of what is in his mind already, who wants his own features 'reflected flatteringly back', is the vigilant guardian of what Boothby calls 'a stable and predictable identity'. What I think is worth adding to this account – and one that is left out of most accounts of repression – is that this fictional character called the ego is acting with extraordinary omniscience when these impulses are repressed. It is as if the ego already knows exactly what will disrupt this apparently secure identity; that the ego knows with astounding epistemological certainty both the nature of this identity and, indeed, the nature of the desire, and about what will happen if there was to be any kind of contact or even exchange between them. The assumption is of catastrophe rather than of modification or even enrichment (Greene's adult reader ventures the possibility of modifying 'some views we already hold'). One wants to get out of something only when one presumes that one knows what is going to happen if one doesn't. Wanting to get out, in other words, then, whatever else it is – and it may be essential for survival – is all too easily a form of omniscience. We want to get out before we know what it is we are getting out of. At its most extreme, this is what we call a phobia.

Indeed, one of the situations in which we seem to know more about the experiences we don't have than about the experiences we do have is when we get out of something. When I get out of a relationship – when I repress my impulse – I act as if I know what would happen if I don't do this. But I am talking about an experience that I haven't in fact had. I can never know what would have happened if I had stayed in the relationship, I can only imagine it. But with the repressed desire it is, of course, different; the desire has been felt, has been recognized as an urge to action, but then repressed into an internal world where it remains, in Boothby's term, as an 'incipient' act. In its state of repression it is an uncompleted action, a thus far missed opportunity. Though the ego, our more conscious self, is living as if it knows exactly what would happen were this impulse to be enacted. Faced with unacceptable desires, the ego is in a continual state of performance anxiety. We know exactly what would happen if we did the unacceptable thing, and we have no idea. I know more about the experiences I haven't had than about the experiences I have had; and yet this knowledge is no more and no less than a rationale for repression. Getting out of something involves a prediction of what will happen if we stay; and this prediction is always a story about what we will miss out on. It is Freud's view that we are excessively disturbed by what we will miss out on if we try to enact an unacceptable desire.

Graham Greene's novel of 1951, *The End of the Affair*, is a story about two people – a novelist, Maurice Bendrix, and a married woman, Sarah Miles – trying to get out of a love affair with each other, in wartime London. Bendrix has got out of fighting in the war because he has a disability, a limp. Because Bendrix is a writer, and the writer-narrator of the novel, the reader's attention is continually drawn throughout the book to the relationship between writing and avoidance. If you call a novel *The End of the Affair* and the first sentence of the novel is: 'A story has no beginning or end: arbitrarily one chooses that moment of experience from which to look back or from which to look ahead'; and the narrator goes on to doubt whether 'one chooses' at all, then you are warning the reader to trust neither the teller nor the tale. Is the narrator trying to get out of what we call responsibility for his story? It may not be the end of the affair, even though the woman is dead by the end of the book, and what we are being told at the start of the novel may not be the beginning of the story, but simply, arbitrarily, where the book begins.

Greene, of course, is a writer virtually obsessed by betrayal, by untrustworthiness, by false promises; but he is a writer shrewd enough to know that betrayal only matters because something else matters more. 'To render the highest justice to corruption you must retain your innocence,' he wrote in an essay on Henry James in 1936; 'you have to be conscious all the time within yourself of treachery to something valuable.' A treacherous act is one in which you get yourself out of something – call it an agreement, tacit or otherwise. *The End of the Affair*, which is full of treacherous, and possibly treacherous, moments, begins with a get-out clause. It says, in effect: I will tell you a story about the end of an affair, but it may not be the end, and where it starts may not be the beginning. 'Marry me: threat or promise?' Christopher Ricks once began a review of John Updike's *Marry Me*. Don't trust me, or the story is the threat and the promise of Greene's anti-romance, in which the romance is the 'something valuable' that he can't get round. *The End of the Affair* is Greene's attempt to corrupt the innocent childlike believer in stories and their promise. And it is about two people trying to get out of a love affair, one while it is still going on and one when it is over.

There is a scene late in the novel when Bendrix goes to the cremation of his ex-lover Sarah with a young woman he has, as it were, picked up on the way, who he believes he can easily seduce. The girl, Sylvia, is only too happy to lie to her boyfriend, Waterbury, in order to be with Bendrix. But suddenly at the funeral Bendrix is overcome with dread about the situation he has created. His seduction begins to backfire.

Hate lay like boredom over the evening ahead. I had committed myself: without love I would have to go through the gestures of love. I felt the guilt before I had committed the crime, the crime of drawing the innocent into my own maze. The act of sex may be nothing, but when you reach my age you learn that at any time it may prove to be everything. I was safe, but who could tell to what neurosis in this child I might appeal? At the end of the evening I would make love clumsily, and my very clumsiness, even my impotence if I proved impotent, might do the trick, or I would make love expertly, and my experience too might involve her. I implored Sarah, Get me out of this, get me out of it, for her sake, not mine.

. . . [Sylvia] stood there in her black trousers, among the frozen puddles, and I thought, this is where a whole long future may begin. I implored Sarah, Get me out of it. I don't want to begin it all again and injure her. I'm incapable of love. Except of you, except of you . . .

Bendrix is convinced that he knows, not what will happen if he goes to bed with Sylvia now, but the range of possibilities of what might happen. In his account Sylvia is a cipher; having met her once, a short time ago that day, he seems to know a great deal about her; or rather, generically, about women and sexuality. And interestingly his omniscience here is all about his own omnipotence; if he makes love clumsily it might do the trick, and if he makes love expertly, that 'too might involve her'. There is no suggestion that she might change his plans, that who she happens to be might impinge upon the certainties of his fantasy. Imploring Sarah to get him out – delegating his agency to her, even in her absence – seems to come out of an uncontestable knowledge about himself and about Sylvia; about an experience neither of them have yet had. The question is, what might happen in the absence of such certainties? It is possible, for example, that one gets out of something – that Bendrix needs to get out of being with Sylvia, with whom 'a whole long future may begin' – because there is something he doesn't want to know (just as, for the narrator of 'This Be the Verse', there may be all sorts of things he doesn't want to know about himself that having children would expose). Why do we seem to know more about the experiences we don't have than about the ones that we do have?

Because only this makes the getting-out possible, and because it is deprivation that makes us imagine. What Freud called 'trial action in thought' is the 'what if' born of the wish for satisfaction. We are seduced by the plausibility born of fear. Omniscience is a pretext and an alibi. In this scenario, we get out before we know what we are getting out of. The project, one might say, is to not know what one is getting out of. The get-out clause precedes the experience.

There is, of course, a Freudian banality in all this because desire is always conflictual – and always smacks of the forbidden. We all live by our get-out clauses. And yet Bendrix's experience, refracted through the language of psychoanalysis, has something to add to all this. It is what the psychoanalyst André Green calls (as I quoted earlier) 'the permanent dialectic between misrecognition and recognition in psychic work', the attempt at satisfaction without turning into someone too unacceptable to oneself, or into something unacceptable to the ego.

'Occultation' – André Green's word for the way in which we obscure ourselves – which means 'hiding', also has 'occult' in it, which might suggest the mystifying of experience, the adding of mystery to experience by hiding from it (getting out can make what you are getting out of seem supernatural). The acceptable image of oneself, which one is so busily constructing and sustaining, may of course be a 'bad' image. Greene himself, a writer perhaps overcommitted, as it were, to the idea of original sin, was obsessed by that apparent contradiction, of getting away from oneself. Whatever one can get out of, one can't get out of one's putative nature. In the Preface to the appropriately entitled *Ways of Escape* Greene writes that he has included pieces

> on some of the troubled places in the world where I have found myself involved for no good reason, though I can see now that my travels, as much as the act of writing, were ways of escape. As I have written elsewhere in this book, 'Writing is a form of therapy; sometimes I wonder how all those who do not write, compose or paint can manage to escape the madness, the melancholia, the panic fear which is inherent in the human condition.' Auden noted: 'Man needs escape as he needs food and deep sleep.'

At the point at which he is writing about ways of escape Greene escapes, as it were, into quoting himself, and then Auden. It is an odd picture of both art and therapy; they are ways of escaping – not confronting, not transforming, not understanding, not defying – 'the madness, the melancholia, the panic fear' that are deemed to be integral to human nature. The certainty of knowing what one is escaping from is one of the misrecognitions required to construct an acceptable image of oneself. Getting out involves, whatever else it involves, not going on looking at what you don't want to see.

Even though the phrase implies it, it would be absurd to think that whenever we are 'getting out of it' we are merely skiving, simply or solely evading or avoiding something. As the psychoanalyst Michael Balint once remarked, in a glancing criticism of Freudianism, whenever we are running away from something we are always running towards something else. It may, for example, be a good question to ask of any text, or indeed of any theory (like psychoanalysis): what does it get you out of? Not just what does it get you out of having to believe, or abide by, but what mood, what state of mind does it release you from? Not, what can you get out of this book? But, what can it get you out of? If reading can be, in the best sense, escapist, then it might help one discover what it is one wants to get away from. And this would be, to use Harold Bloom's language, a swerve towards a pragmatic criticism. 'I prefer to ask the pragmatic question,' Bloom writes in *Agon*, 'what is it that we want our tropes to do for us?' 'The language of American criticism,' he continues,

> ought to be pragmatic and outrageous, or perhaps I verge on saying that American pragmatism, as Rorty advises, always asks of a text: what is it good for, what

can I do with it, what can it do for me, what can I make
it mean? I confess that I like these questions, and they
are what I think strong reading is all about, because
strong reading doesn't ever ask: Am I getting this poem
right? Strong reading *knows* that what it does to the
poem is right, because it knows what Emerson, its
American inventor, taught it, which is that the true ship
is the shipbuilder. If you don't believe in your reading
then don't bother anyone else with it, but if you do,
then don't care also whether anyone else agrees with
it or not.

Bloom makes a virtue of misrecognition, and prioritizes,
in his Freudian way, what the reader needs from the
poem, and so what the reader needs the poem for. In
Bloom's account the question 'Am I getting this poem
right?' is as misleading as the question 'Am I right to
have this need?' The questions that Rorty asks of a text
and that Bloom 'confesses' to like – 'what is it good for,
what can I do with it, what can it do for me, what can
I make it mean?' – turn the text into a new-found tool;
but unlike a hammer or a saw, its form does not dictate
its function; what determines its function is what the
reader wants it for. And the reason the strong reader
is not seeking agreement or consensus for his reading
is because no one can tell you that you don't need
what you claim to need, they can tell you only that you
shouldn't; just as no one can tell you that the joke that

amuses you isn't funny, they can tell you only that you shouldn't be amused by it.

But the outrageous, pragmatic strong reader in this account reads as if he knows what he wants, and not as though he is conflicted about what he wants, or indeed is in flight from it (he might, of course, discover it through the reading). The strong reader's belief in his reading is such that he does not need to persuade or convert anyone else. But by negating the contribution of others, the strong reader misses out on being told what his strong reading might be, in the best and the worst sense, an attempt to get out of. Rorty's questions might be rephrased as: What is the text good for getting me out of? What can I use it to get out of? What can I make it mean in order to free me of a previously confining belief or desire? The pragmatist who knows and wants to find out what he doesn't want, but doesn't need to know in the same way, with the same certainty, what he really does want, says to the text: get me out of here. A lot depends on whether we construct an acceptable image of ourselves around knowing what we don't want or knowing what we do want.

When Freud remarked in 'The Disposition to Obsessional Neurosis' (1913) that we should 'derive the capacity for the origin of morality from the fact that in the order of development hate is the precursor of love', he was suggesting that wanting to get out of it – for example, out of a relationship with a needed other person – is always prior to wanting to get into it; and the 'it', in this context, is what we call a relationship. If hate is the precursor of love, then getting out of relationships is the precursor of getting into them; and this, Freud suggests, is the origin of morality. Love starts from hate. The precursor of love is knowing what we don't want, what we want to get out of. It is not surprising, though it needs to be teased out, why this should be the origin of morality, at least in Freud's view. In my version of strong reading, the strong reader is trying to rediscover what he hates, and he is looking for clues about how he can get out of it.

It is a paradoxical idea that the human subject begins by trying to get out of having what we call relationships, exchanges, with others; that he gets into relationships only by trying to get out of them. That, as we shall see, in at least one of Freud's envisionings of this, we are by inclination self-satisfying and self-satisfied creatures forced to acknowledge our dependence on others. It is, in this picture, in our nature to act against our nature. Our need for others is a kind of defeat or capitulation: the submission that turns into our most difficult admission. Freudian Man, as he was once called, can get into things – or at least get into the things that he most desires – only by trying to get out of them. The way in is through the out door; avoiding things is a way of attending to them, of keeping them in mind. Freud's mechanisms of defence, like Bloom's revisionary ratios, are confrontations through avoidance, the getting out of a dependence that is experienced as an indebtedness, or of a desire that is experienced as an enthralment. Freud invites us to wonder what relationships would be like if we dropped the idea that they had anything to do with indebtedness or obligation.

And yet, even as we formulate this in the reductive language of modern hedonism, as the avoidance of pain and the seeking of pleasure, one thing is abundantly clear: there is no more fundamental picture of the human subject than as a creature trying to get out of something. If getting out of it has come to suggest evasive cowardice – a weakness, a failing – we may wonder, at least from the available pictures of human nature, what is implied when we are not getting out of something or other.

There is no subject to which the literary arts are more devoted; literature is escapist, whatever else it is, in its incessant descriptions of people trying to release themselves from something or other. It is not just, as Sartre said, and as I quoted earlier, that 'genius' is the word we use for people who get themselves out of impossible situations; but that literary geniuses, as well as people not so talented, write about people getting themselves out of impossible situations. If all novels, as Tony Tanner once suggested, are about adultery, then they are all about people getting out of something that has become unbearable. As are Genesis, all Greek tragedies, all the great epic poems, all of Shakespeare's plays, and so on. Wanting to get out of it is not, in this sense, news; or, perhaps, it is the news that stays news, i.e., the eternal personal and political project. Psychoanalysis, one might say, is a modern formalization of the ultimate modern predicament, as is Marxism. 'Men are always trying to get away in one piece,' one of Grace Paley's characters remarks. And perhaps all of us are just trying to get away in as many pieces as are required. Required, that is, by the cultures in which we have grown up.

The triangle of principal characters in *The End of the Affair* are all saying 'get me out of here', and 'here' is their ineluctable human nature. And yet, of course, a novelist who believes in original sin, and begins his novel, which also believes in it, 'A story has no beginning or end', is casting his theology into doubt at the outset. The narrator of 'This Be the Verse' begins his verse with 'They fuck you up, your mum and dad', and yet clearly they don't fuck you up in a way that precludes getting out as a positive project (or pre-empts the value of writing and publishing the poem). And Bloom's pragmatic strong reader, like his strong poet, is quite clearly and actively defying the past that intimidates him. In each of my three (post-war) examples, there is an undoing of determinisms. And this is done, paradoxically, through a supposed omniscience about the past. Those who cannot pretend to know everything about the past are doomed to repeat it. We can get out only by presuming an omniscience about what we are getting out of; which is always, whatever else it is, an omniscience about the satisfactions we seek. And it is the written, spoken and sung arts – the verbal arts – that are the arts of omniscience. Only in words is anyone ever omniscient. And omniscience, as we shall see, is the enemy, the saboteur, of satisfaction.

On Satisfaction

The way through the world
Is more difficult to find than the way beyond it.

Wallace Stevens, 'Reply to Papini'

By the end of a tragedy the tragic hero discovers that he had the wrong picture of his satisfaction; or, rather, that is what is revealed about the tragic hero, whether or not he realizes it. There was something he believed would satisfy him – that in the most fundamental sense he wanted, or believed he wanted – and in the pursuit of it he destroys himself, and wreaks more general havoc. Lear, Othello, Macbeth are stark instances of what Wittgenstein famously referred to as being 'bewitched' by a picture. They knew so certainly what they wanted partly because it is impossible to have a wish without having a picture of its satisfaction; desire always comes with this picture attached; though it is often a tacit picture, as it were, an unconscious one. A picture rendered unconscious by the exigencies of reality. Satisfaction has always happened in our minds before we are satisfied; satisfaction comes first, that is to say, as a form of truth (states of conviction are the closest we come, as adults, to this initial fantasy of satisfaction). It is as though in fantasy wanting always brings with it a guarantee; not always that there will be satisfaction, but of what satisfaction will be like when it comes. Or what the satisfaction will be like – what Oedipus and the state will be like after the criminal has been found – is taken for granted. It is an assumed good. Our doubts tend to be about whether we can get the satisfactions that we seek, not about the nature of these satisfactions. *Othello* is particularly interesting in this regard because no one in the play doubts what it is they want, they doubt only whether they have the wherewithal to get it.

Desire is inextricable – literally inconceivable, unintelligible – without an imagining of its possible satisfaction, even though states of satisfaction are peculiarly resistant to articulation. The language of satisfaction is notably impoverished, riddled with clichés and exclamations, 'that was amazing' and so on. But one of the strange things about satisfaction is that its anticipation precedes its realization; that it happens twice – not quite the first time as farce and the second time as tragedy – but first wishfully (in fantasy) and then in reality, if one is lucky. Satisfaction is looked forward to before it happens – we have the experience in our minds before we have the experience – and this looking forward makes all the difference to what can happen. When we wait too long for someone we are looking forward to seeing, we see them differently; often we see them, at least in the first instance, as not worth looking forward to.

In what Freud called 'primary process thinking,' the wish is conceived of as gratified, it comes in gratifying form; in 'secondary process thinking,' reality is taken into account. 'The strangest characteristic of unconscious (repressed) processes,' Freud writes in 'Formulations on the Two Principles of Psychic Functioning', 'results from their total disregard for reality-testing; thought-reality is equated with external reality, the wish with its fulfilment'; 'the pleasure-ego,' he writes, 'can do nothing but *wish* . . . the reality-ego has no other task than to strive for what is *useful* and to protect itself from what is harmful.' The 'pleasure-ego' – ourselves in our unconscious fantasy life – is an omnipotent, satisfied hedonist; the 'reality-ego' is a pragmatist.

In other words, the satisfaction has always already happened in fantasy. So, at least unconsciously, there is nothing about which we are more certain than the nature of our satisfactions; or, to put it another way, Freud describes how much work we do to ensure that our satisfaction is no surprise. And this leaves us with a paradox, which has to take the form of a question: when you already know what satisfaction is, how can you possibly find out what it is like?

A picture of satisfaction, we might say then, at least to begin with, is a flight from wanting; a refuge from the rigours and risks of desire; a refuge, in fact, from real satisfaction. In fantasy, in the wishing scene, we leapfrog over the obstacles, or rather we don't succumb to them (even though, or because, in Barthes's telling phrase, 'my body is not a hero'). We fast-forward through the frustrating bits. In Bion's language we 'evade' frustration rather than 'modifying' it. Our fantasies of satisfaction – our preconceptions about satisfaction – are where we hide from the possibility of real satisfaction. 'Straight satisfy yourself', Roderigo says to Brabantio in the first scene of *Othello*, as though it was as simple as that; as though there was something Brabantio could immediately go and do to prove that he knows his daughter and her whereabouts. Straight satisfy yourself. That is the first thought, and it is a fateful wish. When Brabantio does this, what is satisfied in him – his wish to know about Desdemona, to know about her desire – leads to a greater and more vengeful frustration, a bitter defeatedness: 'It is too true an evil: gone she is; / And what's to come of my despised time / Is nought but bitterness.' Everything happens very quickly in *Othello* – that is to say, people believe and claim to know things about each other very quickly – as people do in fantasy. Fantasy is the medium in which we jump to conclusions. And the conclusions we jump to are about satisfaction, and are themselves satisfying.

Imagining satisfaction is a way of not thinking about wanting, not thinking about the experience of wanting.

As though wanting itself is in some way unbearable; as though there is something about it we would rather not know about (or do). The satisfaction scene replaces an uncertainty with a certainty; in Freud's terms, a 'positive hallucination replaces a negative hallucination', bad things are made to look good (patience is its own reward, and so on). The something about wanting that is unbearable is transformed into the something about being satisfied that works. We need pictures of satisfaction to make bearable, to make plausible, to make attractive, to make viable, our desiring. They are like adverts for desiring. How strange this is; the ways in which fantasy at once blackmails or seduces or lures us into going through with our wanting, and at the same time pre-empts our going through with it; that we have to do this to ourselves, as though we are at best resistant and at worst phobic of wanting, of acknowledging our wants. We have to be attentive, in other words, to what we use fantasy to do; whether it becomes, as we say, an end in itself. It is uncanny to be an animal that doesn't want to do the real work of wanting; pragmatic and Darwinian, in that wanting can endanger one, but strange in the way the solutions become more of the problem. Solutions becoming more of the problem, of course, is one definition of neurosis. Every time someone solves a problem in *Othello*, they create a bigger problem for themselves, whether they realize it or not; that is, until the very end of the play when the consequences of the tragedy are unknown. As we shall see, when satisfaction is invoked in *Othello*, and by Othello himself, what is being sought is proof and revenge, knowledge and retaliation, certainty and redress. And what is more than intimated, as I want to show, is just how inextricable these things can be.

Satisfaction, certainty and revenge. There is the uncertainty, the risk of wanting, and the strange – uncanny – kind of knowledge that comes with it, of the want met, of the wished-for state achieved, or summoned. The picture of how wanting will turn out, the ideal masquerading as the real. Pornography and romantic fantasy – and their derivatives in so-called higher culture – are pictures of people achieving a rendezvous with their apparently wished-for satisfactions. The whole notion of satisfaction, in other words, brings with it, in its wake, a knot of inevitable preoccupations. These can be briefly stated by giving the first three entries for 'satisfy' in the *OED*: '1. to pay off or discharge fully (a debt, obligation); to comply with (a demand); 2. to make compensation or reparation for (a wrong injury) . . . to make atonement; 3. to make satisfaction, full payment, reparation or atonement . . . (said of Christ)'. The psychoanalyst, unsurprisingly perhaps, pricks up her ears here; unsurprisingly because satisfaction, or something about satisfaction – not everything about it – is the heart of the matter of psychoanalysis. For 'indebtedness' the psychoanalyst can read 'dependence'; for 'comply with (a demand)' one might read Winnicott; for 'reparation' one might read Klein; for 'to make satisfaction' and to 'discharge fully' – and indeed for the idea of making 'full payment' or not – one might read Freud.

It is the link between satisfaction and redress – the idea that a satisfaction scene, whatever else it is, is a revenge tragedy – that I want to pursue; and the sense that we waylay our desire – make it literally unreal – with pictures of its satisfaction. Pornography, for example, can easily be used, among many other things, to pre-empt the elaboration of erotic fantasy; it can be, in Masud Khan's words, 'the stealer of dreams'. To put it in old-fashioned Freudian language, fantasies of satisfaction are defences against desiring, the attempt in fantasy to take the risk out of the desire; or to put it in more Kleinian language, fantasies of satisfaction are attacks on desire; they are, in fact, against desiring, both up against it and in opposition to it. Our fantasies of satisfaction are clues to our fears about desiring. Wishful fantasies are the original sins of omission.

So we have to start imagining desiring not without an object of desire, but without imagining too certainly the satisfactions that might accrue, not being too quick to satisfy ourselves in fantasy; and, when we do, being able to ironize such satisfactions (not take them too literally, or too solemnly). And doing this, of course, affects our imagining of the object of desire and what we can claim to know about it. We would think about a revolution or a wedding very differently if we had too little knowledge of what would occur afterwards, when too little knowledge is what we will always have (this is what the word 'risk' is for); or if we acknowledged that what we know about a revolution or a wedding are the wishes it carries. Tragedies are dramas in which satisfactions are too exactly imagined by their heroes, and then too ruthlessly believed in and pursued (so one cure for tragedy would seem to be the pursuit of falsification; Othello wants Iago to prove to him that Desdemona is unfaithful, not that she isn't); and they are dramas about the consequences of too exactly imagining such things (which means imagining them without irony); of making a satisfaction into a thing (and tragedies are, in this sense, one of the best ways we have of thinking about pornography and romantic fantasy).

'It is not merely an appetite for beauty,' Stanley Cavell writes in *Disowning Knowledge*, 'that produces Othello's most famous image of his victim, as a piece of cold and carved marble (". . . whiter skin of hers than snow, / And smooth as monumental alabaster" [V.ii.4–5])'; 'Where does his image come from?' asks Cavell. I want to ask in turn: what might make someone turn satisfaction into a thing (as though satisfaction was akin to private property, something one could own or keep)? And this is a version of the questions: why is satisfaction always linked with revenge; and why is revenge always linked with certainty? Why are these things so bound up with each other? These are knots in *Othello*, and knots more explicitly, more theoretically, in Freud and in psychoanalysis.

So we can put together here, as a way towards answering these questions, Stanley Cavell's remark 'everyone knows that *something* is mad in the sceptic's fantastic quest for certainty' and Winnicott's comment that it is 'the hallmark of madness when an adult puts too powerful a claim on the credulity of others' (and, we can add, when an adult puts too powerful a claim on his own credulity, as Othello does). 'The fantastic quest for certainty', like the 'too powerful a claim on the credulity of others' and oneself, are descriptions – as Cavell intimates – of a fantasy of wished-for satisfaction; they are certain, that is, apparently guaranteed, and they command assent, that is, we believe them unquestioningly, at least to begin with. Straight satisfy yourself; but how would Brabantio, or anyone, satisfy their wish for knowledge about another person's desire, let alone a daughter's desire? It is worth wondering what happens to our erotic life, or to our sociability with each other and ourselves, when certainty becomes our picture of satisfaction. And what happens to our satisfaction, to our possibilities for satisfaction, when it does. It has indeed become difficult not to imagine satisfaction as having something to do with certainty; and I would add to this that the quest for certainty in certain areas of our lives is a quest for revenge. Not merely a taking revenge on the uncertainties of life, but revenge for the uncertainty built into wanting. Revenge makes wanting definitive. Clearly, our idealization of trust, safety, commitment and continuity (and security) is a symptom of, is a way of acknowledging, that wanting is not a species of prediction.

Suffering, the psychoanalyst Joseph Sandler once remarked in a rather too neat formulation, is a consequence of the distance between the ego and the ego-ideal, the distance between who I feel myself to be and who I want to be. The object of desire may be a political ideal, a personal ambition or a person, but we mind the gap; between us and them, between ourselves as wanting, and lacking, and ourselves as defeated and abject, or not; between the dependent self and what it depends on. And adjustments can be made to narrow the gap or to avoid it, which are all variations on the continual theme of mitigating desire. So-called tragic heroes are by definition people who don't set off wanting something with a view to something else more satisfying turning up along the way. They are not casual or cool or freewheeling or easily distractible or waiting for something to turn up. They are, as we say, determined; overdetermined. They are intent.

'From an analytical point of view,' Lacan writes in the *Ethics Seminar*, 'the only thing of which one can be guilty is of having given ground relative to one's desire'; what tragedy reveals to us is that 'the access to desire necessitates crossing not only all fear but all pity, because the voice of the hero trembles before nothing, and especially not before the good of the other'. How do you know what your desire is? It is that which makes you feel guilty when you betray it; not when you betray someone else, but when you betray yourself; indeed, for Lacan self-betrayal, the self-betrayal of giving up on one's desire, is the source of guilt. We suffer from failures of ruthlessness. The tragic hero for Lacan – and you can almost hear the erotic excitement he feels in the presence of his tragic hero – is exemplary. Only the timid could think of him as flawed (it is difficult also not to hear the voice of the hero trembling 'before nothing, and especially not before the good of the other' as the successful capitalist in a world in which the only real political project is lowering the tax on the rich). But then Lacan, in a more traditional Freudian vein, makes a similar link to Cavell's, between the desire of the tragic hero and the desire for knowledge, in which the hinge is the question of certainty. 'I think that throughout this historical period,' Lacan continues in his blithe, sweeping way,

the desire of man, which has been felt, anaesthetized, put to sleep by moralists, domesticated by educators, betrayed by the academies, has quite simply taken refuge or been repressed in that most subtle and blind-est of passions, as the story of Oedipus shows, the passion for knowledge. That's the passion that's cur-rently going great guns and is far from having said its last word.

One of the ways 'we', in this 'historical period' – and it's not quite clear what this period is or who the 'we' are – have given ground relative to our desire is to have taken refuge from it or repressed it into 'the passion for knowledge'. As if to say, it is not knowledge we really want; or, rather, knowledge is what we start 'really' wanting when we evade (that is, repress) our desire; knowledge is a sublimation. But the tragic hero, as Lacan intimates in his reference to Oedipus, may be precisely the one who *cedes his desire by transforming it into a desire for knowledge*. He gives up on what he originally wanted, and wants knowledge instead. To be-gin with, Oedipus wanted, albeit unconsciously, to kill his father and marry his mother; then, because of the suffering invoked, he wanted to know what happened. So at the beginning, in Lacan's language, Oedipus was the subject of his own desire; but was the Oedipus who wanted to know the subject of his own desire? Is knowing what you have done not having the courage of your unconscious convictions? Certain knowledge is punishment for Oedipus, his revenge, as it were, on himself. So, we might ask, is the psychoanalytic project the individual's revenge on himself through knowledge?

Othello is someone in a need-to-know situation. What may be tragic about the tragic hero is the betrayal of his desire through the certain picturing of its satisfaction that is called knowledge. Indeed, the first sentence of the play – Roderigo's to Iago, 'Tush! Never tell me' – is an accusation that sounds like an order. The play begins with Roderigo accusing Iago of withholding knowledge from him, but in the form of an imperative: never tell me. One thing Othello clearly believes in – that is, knows to exist – is certain knowledge about another person. Very soon Othello doesn't want Desdemona – if he did at all; and Tony Tanner suggests plausibly that if Othello had ever wanted her he would not have been so easily dissuaded by Iago – he wants 'ocular proof', certain knowledge of her infidelity. And it is an extraordinary and horrifying exchange of one object of desire for another; the desire for Desdemona exchanged for the desire to know her as unfaithful and to kill her (Othello, as many people have noted, has a lot more difficulty in trying to kill Iago). 'Giv[ing] ground relative to one's desire' suggests there is something about oneself, called 'desire', which has a certainty about itself, and the tragic hero lives this certainty out as a fate. And that this desire can itself be betrayed – taken refuge from or repressed (that is, transformed into) what Lacan calls 'the passion for knowledge'. Aside from the obvious fact that Lacan has given us this description as a piece of knowledge, the question is raised: is the desire for knowledge, for knowledge of another desired person, itself a betrayal of one's desire, and therefore something one might be permanently guilty about? Or is the representation of satisfaction a betrayal of one's desire? Is the satisfaction scene – which should perhaps be called the satisfaction set-up – a profound misleading, a misfire, a false knowing of another person? As though the way we mis-imagine someone is to imagine the satisfaction they can provide, with such certainty (and this means if they are not providing it they must be withholding it, or giving it to someone else). As though some kinds of knowledge – call them wishful fantasies of satisfaction – were both the preconditions for satisfaction and a satisfaction in their own right; as though certain knowledge was the object of desire. And if this object of desire was a person, our picture of satisfaction would be of some kind of certainty in our relation to them, say, a certainty of their presence, of their availability, of their reliability, of their telling us the truth, of their fidelity; of their being, in short, knowable. The providers, we might say, of certain satisfactions. In a passage from *Disowning Knowledge*, already quoted in this book but worth returning to here, Cavell writes,

Nothing could be more certain to Othello than that
Desdemona exists; is flesh and blood; is separate from
him; other. This is precisely the possibility that tortures
him. The content of his torture is the premonition of
the existence of another, hence of his own, his own
[existence] as dependent and partial . . . His professions
of scepticism over her faithfulness are a cover story for
a deeper conviction; a terrible doubt covering a yet
more terrible certainty, an unstatable certainty . . . this
is what I have throughout kept arriving at as the cause
of scepticism – the attempt to convert the human condition, the condition of humanity, into an intellectual
difficulty, a riddle. (To interpret 'a metaphysical finitude
as an intellectual lack'.)

Dependence, of course, does not start out as a problem
of knowledge. How does it become one? And then, what
happens to satisfaction in the process? *Othello* gives us
a clue, or, rather, a complex drama that psychoanalysis
wants to make explicit; wants to make, that is to say,
a question of knowledge. How does the individual get
from needing to needing to know? And what is the fate
of satisfaction in this drama that psychoanalysis calls
'development'? The child needs; then he needs to know.
It is important to remember, Winnicott once remarked,
that all philosophers were once babies. It is also important
to remember that no baby was once a philosopher. If
babies had a motto it would be 'Straight satisfy yourself.'

It is of interest that it is in *Othello* that Shakespeare uses the word 'satisfy' most frequently; and that to begin with in the play it is Brabantio's satisfaction that is the issue. It is the aggrieved father seeking satisfaction, that is, justice, in relation to his daughter. 'Where will you that I go / To answer this your charge?' Othello asks him directly in Act I, scene 2;

> BRABANTIO: To prison, till fit time
> Of law and course of direct session
> Call thee to answer.
>
> OTHELLO: What if I do obey?
> How may the Duke be therewith satisfied,
> Whose messengers are here about my side,
> Upon some present business of the state
> To bring me to him?

It is worth noting that Othello, in the first instance, in his first use of the word, is not ostensibly concerned with his own satisfaction; the question for him, at that moment, is which of these two senior Venetians he should satisfy. Satisfaction is linked to obligation, to obedience – 'What if I do obey?' – and to what will later be called, in a poignant phrase, 'divided duty'. It is the men, and the state, that need to be satisfied. Othello's dilemma here – a dilemma, as we shall see, integral to the idea of satisfaction – is: who would it be most just for me to satisfy; to whom do I most owe satisfaction? To satisfy, for Othello at this moment, is to give something to someone who is most justly owed it. But is it more just to protect the state or to protect the daughters? Othello is asking here which law should be satisfied (satisfaction meaning the right following of a rule). Othello stages himself as the one who must satisfy, not as the one who must be satisfied. Or the one whose satisfaction is bound up with the satisfying of seniors. But, above all, at the very beginning of *Othello*, satisfaction is seen always to involve competing satisfactions.

When he defends himself, in front of the Duke and Brabantio, Othello refers to other, more obvious satisfactions; and he is keen to reassure them that his relationship with Desdemona is not about those. His love for Desdemona was not 'To please the palate of my appetite, / Nor to comply with heat – the young affects / In me defunct – and proper satisfaction. / But to be free and bounteous to her mind' (I.3). The line 'In me defunct – and proper satisfaction' is assumed to be corrupt in both the folio and the quarto. Whether or not it is, it is an interesting addition or emendation, raising as it does the question of the nature of Othello's satisfaction, which will become all too evident in Act III, scene 3. Here Iago's insistent and terrifying (and terrorizing) question to Othello is, what will satisfy him? And this means, starkly, what will satisfy him: that Desdemona is faithful, or not?

It is partly a question of what counts as evidence, and partly a question of how, when satisfaction is sought – satisfaction of a certain kind – evidence becomes the issue. And in this sense the play links empiricism with desire, and particularly with revenge. The satisfactions of evidence are the satisfactions of making a case, for or against, ideally without straining anyone's credulity. In Freud, satisfaction is such that the individual is always having to make a case for his or her satisfaction, both consciously and unconsciously; the reality-ego, we should remember Freud saying, was interested in the useful, in what works. And perhaps like all legal cases – desiring as an internalized legal case – satisfaction is linked with redress; and so, more or less explicitly, with revenge. The satisfactions of justice are inextricable from the gratifica-tions of sense. Development is the ongoing transition from sensual satisfaction of vital needs and accompanying pleasures to questions of fairness, fidelity and knowledge.

It is Iago who first uses the word in Act III, scene 3, to prey on Othello's mind. 'Did Michael Cassio,' he asks in all apparent innocence – just getting the facts straight – 'when you woo'd my lady, / Know of your love?' Othello: 'He did, from first to last: why dost thou ask?' Iago: 'But for a satisfaction of my thought; / No further harm.' No further harm, as he knows, does further harm, and introduces the idea of satisfying one's thoughts, and by thoughts he means suspicions. Once thought becomes suspicion there is only one kind of satisfaction. What Iago does is destroy the conflict in Othello's mind, reduce the competing satisfactions to one, the proof of her infidelity. Othello very quickly relinquishes the satisfaction of finding Desdemona innocent. What Iago plays on is not exactly the truth about Desdemona, but rather the more disturbing question of what will satisfy Othello (the idea of Desdemona as satisfying Othello is quickly forgotten). In a sense, Othello's satisfaction becomes the problem, not Desdemona; it is almost as if Iago, by reiterating the very word, has made Othello think about his satisfaction for the first time, and it undoes him. Othello, incited by Iago, is made first – and, for the first time in the play, explicitly – to want his satisfaction; and second, to define it. But actually all Othello says is that he wants satisfaction, 'proof', 'a living reason she's disloyal'; he delegates to Iago the description of it.

OTHELLO: By the world.
I think my wife be honest, and think she is not;
I think that thou are just, and think thou art
    not.
I'll have some proof. Her name that was as
    fresh
As Dian's visage is now begrimed and black
As mine own face. If there be cords or
    knives,

> Poison or fire or suffocating streams,
> I'll not endure it. Would I were satisfied!

IAGO: I see, sir, you are eaten up with passion.
     I do repent me that I put it to you.
     You would be satisfied?

OTHELLO: Would! nay, I will.

IAGO: And may. But how? How satisfied, my lord?
     Would you, the supervisor, grossly gape on –
     Behold her topp'd?

OTHELLO: Death and damnation! O!

IAGO: It were a tedious difficulty, I think,
     To bring them to that prospect. Damn them then
     If ever mortal eyes do see them bolster
     More than their own! What then? How then?
     What shall I say? Where's satisfaction?
     It is impossible you should see this,
     Were they as prime as goats, as hot as monkeys,
     As salt as wolves in pride, and fools as gross
     As ignorance made drunk. But yet, I say,
     If imputation and strong circumstances,
     Which lead directly to the door of truth,
     Will give you satisfaction, you may have't.

OTHELLO: Give me a living reason she's disloyal.

Whatever else happens in this dialogue that is an assisted monologue, we see and hear someone, Iago, constituting someone else's desire; or, rather, the nature of their satisfaction. Othello moves very quickly from 'Would I were satisfied' to 'Would! nay, I will' to 'Give me a living reason she's disloyal'; within twenty or so lines, Othello is saying, after Iago's description of Cassio's supposed dream, 'this denoted a foregone conclusion'. And what seems to get him there so quickly is Iago's suggesting so luridly what might satisfy him. 'How satisfied, my lord? / Would you, the supervisor, grossly gape on – / Behold her topp'd?' All Iago does is insistently ask Othello questions about satisfaction, and about his satisfaction; it is, as we say, abstract and concrete, distanced and immediate. 'You would be satisfied?' . . . 'But how? How satisfied, my lord?' . . . 'Where's satisfaction?' . . . 'If imputation and strong circumstances, / Which lead directly to the door of truth, / Will give you satisfaction, you may have't.' Once Othello is so forced to think of satisfaction he can think only of revenge and murder.

It is worth noting that in the subplot of Iago helping Roderigo to get to Desdemona satisfaction is quite openly linked to the giving of reasons. Urging him to kill Cassio, Roderigo says to Iago, 'I will hear further reason for this,' to which Iago replies – and the audience by Act IV have been woken to the word – 'And you shall be satisfied.' And Roderigo furthers the point by saying at the beginning of Act V, 'I have no great devotion to the deed; / And yet he hath given me satisfying reasons.' Reasons are satisfying, and can be the preconditions for satisfaction. 'Give me a living reason she's disloyal,' Othello asked Iago. Giving reasons – in the several senses of 'reasons' – and satisfaction are somehow inextricable, the play keeps telling us. Satisfaction exists in what philosophers call 'the space of reasons', what Robert Brandom in *Reason in Philosophy* calls 'the social practices of giving and asking for reasons'. Satisfaction has its reasons, and without them it isn't possible; and the satisfaction requiring such reasons, in *Othello*, is the satisfaction of murdering a rival male or a frustrating woman. Satisfaction linked to entitlement.

In *Othello* it is extraordinary what the characters are satisfied by, and how they go about seeking satisfaction. What is satisfying – for both Othello and Iago, who are in some way twinned – is legitimating revenge and taking it; finding living reasons and using these as forms of entitlement. Making the case for revenge and carrying it through is satisfying; perhaps one fundamental form of satisfaction. Certainly all of Shakespeare's tragedies – perhaps all tragedies – are about the misfortune of finding good-enough reasons for revenge. To put it another way: tragedies occur when people get their sense of entitlement wrong. The question then arises, is it possible to be wrong about one's entitlement?

And if so, where do the criteria for this wrongness come from? Is it possible to have a realistic sense of entitlement – especially when class distinctions begin to blur – entitlement always being, one way or another, an entitlement to certain satisfactions? And what, if anything, might psychoanalytic stories about pleasure and so-called development have to add to the link between entitlement and satisfaction?

The thing that *Othello* draws us into – and which makes patent a link with Freud, and indeed is something one might say that psychoanalysis has carried on the conversation about – is the notion not simply that revenge is satisfying, but that satisfaction may be vengeful – a more disturbing idea. The Oedipus story, for example, gives us a way of describing the necessary pleasures of revenge, as does *Othello*; but where can we go for the idea that satisfaction may be intrinsically, or partly, vengeful? Well, we can go for half the answer to certain psychoanalytic stories about what is called, ineptly, perversion. Is my satisfaction revenge on the people who have frustrated me? Is my loyalty to people a defence against my being disillusioned by them? For Iago and Othello the satisfaction they seek is revenge on the people who have frustrated them; for Desdemona (in relation to Othello), and for Othello (in relation to Iago), one could surmise that they are so relentlessly loyal as a way of not acknowledging their respective catastrophic disillusionments.

Othello has not turned out to be quite the man Desdemona married, and Iago is not quite as honest as Othello had assumed. There are, we might say, certain disillusionments that tragic heroes (and heroines) can't acknowledge; indeed, the plays are stories about the consequences of unacknowledged or uncompleted disillusionments. And this might be one link with what psychoanalysis has to say; from a psychoanalytic point of view each stage of development turns on a disillusionment – birth on the disillusionment of unity, weaning on the disillusionment of not controlling the object of need, the Oedipus complex on the disillusionment of the nothing that comes from not being all, adolescence with the disillusionment with the parents' authority and sexual and emotional desirability, and so on. Disillusionment may be tragic, may, rather, have its tragic side, but the true havoc of tragedy, from a psychoanalytic point of view, is of disillusionment avoided. It is not that Desdemona is unfaithful; it is, as Cavell intimates, that Othello can't bear to acknowledge that she is not under his remote control. When the ordinary catastrophic disillusionments are repressed, they return with a vengeance. When Paradise is lost, people can't just move on.

'The problem,' Richard Rorty once wrote, 'is that love (and therefore courage and cowardice, sacrifice and selfishness) looks different after one has read Freud.'

And so, by the same token, does disillusionment, and the subsequent re-illusionment to which it can lead (this is what the last moments of the last scenes of tragedies are for, revisioning). In *Othello* this revisioning has to begin with a telling of the story we have just witnessed; 'Myself will straight aboard,' Lodovico says in the last lines of the play, 'and to the state / This heavy act with heavy heart relate' (V.2). As if to say, we have to both continue and start again in the light of these truths. We can't afford to go on living as if certain things are true; we can't afford to live as if Iago or indeed Othello are trustworthy, or trustworthy servants of the state. What we learn from experience is that experience keeps stripping us of dearly held beliefs, about ourselves and others. We can't afford to live as though certain things are true about ourselves. Our satisfactions have to be realigned.

Once, of course, our satisfactions were provided by our parents, or the people who looked after us when we were young. And it is clearly a very significant moment, or series of moments, in a child's life when he begins to notice that there are satisfactions outside the family. This can feel to the child like a murder of the parents, like an act of outrageous and frightening ruthlessness. Or, as the philospher Annette Baier writes (in *Reflections on How We Live*) in a new twist on the perennial theme, 'Parental love, paternal or maternal, is as dangerous a central concept for ethics as is expert wisdom'; because it leads to the perversion of authority called authoritarianism, morality as moralism. In her essay 'The Moral Perils of Intimacy' she returns us to what in the psychoanalytic literature is called the 'problem of perversion'. 'What, after all, did Freud teach us about love?' she asks:

> That it begins in dependency, that its first object is the more powerful but loving mother who has been the loving infant's whole world, and who remains the source of nourishment, security and pleasure. The pathologies of love all develop from this initial situation of unequal dependency. Mother love, if it is to be good of its kind, has to avoid both exploitation of the mother's immensely superior power and that total self-abnegation that turns the infant into a tyrant. Love between unequals in power is good of its kind when it prepares the less powerful one for love between equals. It fails when what it produces is either a toleration of prolonged unequal dependency, or a fear of any dependency, rather than a readiness for reciprocal and equal dependency.

This is a true and useful description until it becomes unduly pastoral; until it provides too wishful a satisfaction scene. Another way of saying this is that the word 'unequal' makes sense in a way that the word 'equal' does not. It may be a disillusionment, but it is a salutary one, that love can never be between equals because love makes people unequal. It returns them to, it reminds them of, an initiating inequality. Love is the medium in which people become unequal, and for the reasons actually spelled out by Baier; the original situation of unequal dependency (or, as the analyst Enid Balint remarked many years ago, the mother is everything to the infant, but the infant is not everything to the mother). It matters hugely, as Baier says, whether and in what ways the mother exploits her 'immensely superior power'; but we all begin in this constitutive predicament of unequal dependency. So when we love, this unequal dependency, and our self-cures for it, are what we return to, what we have recourse to. Our repertoire of ways of loving always includes inequality. All the so-called pathologies come, we might say, from the wish to get even; from the wish to turn the tables; from the wish to revenge ourselves on this first natural order; as a false solution to a fact of life (indeed, it is part of the function of revenge to obscure the nature of the problem it is supposedly a solution to). The aim is to never feel this unequal dependence again (which is Othello's wish), or to only, always and grudgingly feel it, and so try to reverse it (as Iago seems to do). Whether we are superior or servile, sadistic or masochistic, these are solutions to the first predicament, when there was one source of satisfaction. First there was the one and then there were the many. What Baier calls the 'exploitation of the mother's immensely superior power' – or this as the child's experience whether or not it was the mother's intent – is taken to be the precondition of what the psychoanalyst Robert Stoller refers to as 'perversion'. What we have to wonder is whether superior power is not always experienced as exploitation; or conversely what could such unequal power be transformed into? 'Perversion, the erotic form of hatred,' Stoller writes in *Perversion*,

> is a fantasy, usually acted out but occasionally restricted to a daydream (either self-produced or packaged by others, that is, pornography). It is a habitual, preferred aberration necessary for one's full satisfaction, primarily motivated by hostility . . . The hostility in perversion takes form in a fantasy of revenge hidden in the actions that make up the perversion and serves to convert childhood trauma to adult triumph.

As with Annette Baier's account of mothering, we have to, by induction, infer the preferred norm or ideal from the described pathology. In Baier it was love between equals, an intolerance of 'prolonged unequal dependence' and a tolerance of dependence, leading to 'reciprocal and equal dependency' that was the preferred version. In Stoller the preferred version is not dissimilar; the quasi-pastoral idea of mutuality is invoked again, a magical and therefore misleading word. In non-perverse desire there is, presumably, no habitual, necessary aberration, motivated by hostility, and essential for one's full satisfaction; and non-perverse desire is not vengeful. What Stoller adds is a reason for the revenge; it is the attempt 'to convert childhood trauma to adult triumph'. The childhood trauma Stoller is referring to is akin to Baier's account of the 'exploitation of the mother's immensely superior power'. Childhood trauma is the consequence of the uses and abuses of early dependency; and what Stoller calls 'trauma' may be simply another word for 'childhood'; childhood being the cumulative trauma of the inevitable suffering of unequal dependence; the idea of equality prompted by this ineluctable first fact. We should perhaps be searching for better versions of unequal dependency than for the eradication of this particular inequality; or for different forms of satisfaction. The precondition for what Stoller calls 'full satisfaction' for all of us, to varying extents, is revenge.

But what returning the problem to its supposed source in mother-child relations reveals is that revenge is itself a form of magic. There is no redress for the initial and initiating inequality; there is only the illusion of triumph over it – another kind of magic (all magic can ever produce is more magic). In this story the adult ends up enacting a child's view of what it is to be an adult. All triumphs over the object are attempted triumphs over one's need for the object. And all triumphs over one's need for the object are compromised forms of satisfaction. Satisfaction must be felt to be very precarious if it requires such strenuous devices (such elaborate sex-aids); and the person seeking such satisfactions must be very knowing about the satisfactions he seeks, and the preconditions for their possibility. What Stoller calls 'full satisfaction' sounds something of a strain; hemmed in by intractable certainties. Like revenge. This is what I need for full satisfaction. No surprises there. 'Straight satisfy yourself' makes sense only if you know what you are looking for. It is about, in Iago's words, how to 'give satiety a fresh appetite' (II.i). Or how to give ourselves a fresh appetite for satisfaction. Stoller and Baier intimate that there are those lucky ones for whom satisfaction is not revenge.

So, to put it as schematically as possible: from a psychoanalytic point of view, it is when the child waits that he first begins to fantasize, and first begins to think that he knows. In his frustration he pictures his satisfaction; he, as psychoanalysts put it, imagines the breast when he is hungry as a self-cure for the dawning knowledge that he does not control the object who can satisfy him. Frustration can be borne only through a picture of satisfaction; in this account, knowledge is about frustration, about what is felt to be missing or lacking or absent. The child is hungry, fantasizes the breast, and if the mother is sufficiently reliable and comes sooner rather than later, the child has a sense of certainty about his imagined knowledge; he is hungry, he fantasizes the breast, and it arrives; this is called trust. (Of course when we are adults and are sexually desirous, the same principle does not prevail.) If the child is hungry and fantasizes the breast and it doesn't come, the child conceives another kind of certain knowledge; this is called hatred and despair and revenge. In this schema there are two stages in the child's relationship to satisfaction; what we might call two formative pieces of knowledge, which are at the same time disillusionments. First, what satisfies you is in the gift of someone else (which might make you envious); and second, what satisfies you is available to someone else before you, and has to be shared (which will make you jealous and rivalrous). There is no satisfaction without an initiating frustration; and so there is no satisfaction that is not preceded – and to some extent pre-empted – by a wishedfor fantasy of satisfaction (satisfaction begins as truly satisfying but wholly unreal). When T. S. Eliot writes of Othello (in *Shakespeare and the Stoicism of Seneca*) that he is 'endeavouring to escape reality, he has ceased to think about Desdemona, and is thinking about himself', we might redescribe 'thinking about himself' as thinking only about his fantasy of satisfaction. And, as *Othello* makes abundantly clear, there is no satisfaction without conflict; or indeed without conflicting satisfactions. It is easy to see, given the assault course that is satisfaction, why certainties are sought and revenge taken. Or, to put it slightly differently, why states of conviction and revenge are our preferred self-cures; the ways we restore ourselves by magically concealing our dependence on independent others for our satisfaction.

But there is something else worth noticing here, which is that if certain knowledge and revenge are self-cures for the problem of inevitable frustration, they are also, by the same token, self-cures for satisfaction. They are satisfactions conjured as substitutes for – as poor sublimations of – the possibilities of full or realer satisfactions. The ways we cure ourselves of frustration are the ways we cure ourselves of satisfaction. And the ways we cure ourselves of satisfaction are through too knowing, too efficient pictures of our satisfaction. We use satisfactions to cheat us of our satisfactions. We need, in other words, a utopian story about satisfaction running in parallel or concurrently with the anti-utopian story; both, paradoxically, at work in the psychoanalytic account. Whatever else he has done Freud has exposed our avoidance of love as an avoidance of satisfaction. We need, as he suggested, to have better – more interesting, more enlivening, more satisfying – conversations about our frustrations.

Appendix: On Acting Madness

'Acting Madness' was a lecture given at the Brooklyn Academy of Music to introduce a season of three plays – *Macbeth*, *King Lear* and David Holman's dramatization of Gogol's *Diary of a Madman* – on the subject of madness. It was written just after this book was completed, and picks up on many of the book's preoccupations. Madness, and the acting of it, is clearly about frustration, about not getting it, about getting away with it, about getting out of it, and about satisfaction. But 'madness' is also the word we use for a life that has been unlived, or lived in a peculiarly confining way; at least from the point of view of those who think of themselves as sane. Thinking of oneself as sane can be infinitely reassuring, but it can also be radically misleading; and, indeed, distracting. Part of the terror about so-called madness is that it represents one of our unlived lives, something that might have happened to us, something we might have done; something that may have been the only solution to the direst of circumstances. Or even a temptation we had to avoid. When we think of the lives we may have led, there are lives we are relieved to have missed out on, and many more lives perhaps – many more versions of ourselves – that we are not quite so sure about. 'Acting Madness', among other things, is about this distinction, which we are not always able to make.

> In every generation there are quite firm rules on
> how to behave when you are crazy.

> Ian Hacking, *The Social Construction of What?*

My title, 'Acting Madness', was suggested to me, but I took it because it reminded me of Gore Vidal's famous quip about Reagan, that he was 'the acting president'; as if something had happened to the real president and Reagan was temporarily taking his place, standing in for him. There was the real thing, a real president, somewhere – perhaps he was ill or had been kidnapped or even assassinated – but someone had to play his role in the interim. Someone, of necessity, was filling in for him. And, of course, if you have been an actor, as Reagan had been, that might make you better equipped to be an acting president. Or perhaps not? It might make you ham it up, or be too stylized, or so convincingly actorly that people might become suspicious; you might behave as though you were born for the part, that the part was made for you, as a usurper might feel, or an understudy who had got lucky; or indeed a madman such as Gogol's Poprishchin.

It should be noted at the outset that each of the so-called heroes of these three very different plays are wanting to be more powerful than they feel themselves to be, or at least sensing a powerlessness in themselves; they are all troubled by being insufficiently regarded, and begin to act strange as a consequence (and this is remarked upon, just in case we missed it). 'They don't heed me, they don't see me, they don't listen,' Poprishchin shouts out; 'What have I done to them . . . What do they want from poor me – I haven't got anything.' Each has, as it were, a double, a counterpart – a preferred version of themselves, who has more or less everything – with whom they are implicitly making invidious comparisons. Is Lear as loveable as he should be? Has Macbeth 'won' as much as he might ('What he hath lost,' the King says of the Thane of Cawdor in Act I, scene 1, 'noble Macbeth hath won')? Is Poprishchin's true status being recognized initially as a gentleman and ultimately as the King of Spain? These three mad people are seeking solutions to a new-found helplessness; a helplessness we might say that they are at first not quite aware of, and which it is the drama of these three remarkable plays to reveal. A solution is being sought and quickly found for an as-yet-unacknowledged loss; the solution has to be quickly found, otherwise the suffering will start to show, will begin to reveal itself (tragedies expose the quick fix). Great claims are made for the self when it begins to sense its own entropy. At a loss, tremendous gains are proposed. So-called mad people, who are not all the same – just as tragic heroes are not all the same – experience themselves as on the verge of disappearing; they are the always-about-to-be invisible. The person acting madness has to impersonate someone who is quite literally trying to keep up appearances. There is, needless to say, something very theatrical about this. Or, to put it slightly differently, it is a predicament that calls up a certain theatricality.

The fear of losing one's place in other people's minds – the fear of the invisibility of one's need – can summon up the most vivid, the most dramatic performances in oneself. And yet we don't call all the people mad who can make their presence felt, whose 'sentiment of being' (in Rousseau's phrase) is striking. The questions are, what makes us think that someone is mad? What is it about their performance of themselves that makes this the word that occurs to us? Not 'cruel', 'loud', 'abject', 'violent', 'eccentric', 'domineering', 'bizarre', 'mute', 'exploitative', 'inspired', but 'mad'? Who, to ask the obvious question, are the mad being compared with? What is the standard that conjures up the judgement, the particular word? Of course a psychiatrist can answer this question in a way that most of us cannot, which makes the psychiatrist at once both part of the problem and, sometimes, part of the solution. But the idea of someone acting madness might make us want to think something like: as the sane are to the mad, so the actor is to his part. The actor acting madness – in some ways like the mad person himself – has to learn to appear to be mad. But to be mad in a way that holds people's attention; that is, mad in a way that most mad people can never be, but need to be. The mad are people who have never found, or never made, or never had, a sufficiently attentive audience. And this in itself might make us wonder what an audience is for. And remind us that the first audience is the family. And how they responded to our first performances is integral to who we are; and to what we feel about performing. And, indeed, to what we feel about madness.

Vidal's remark about Reagan reminds us of the sense in which the president is also always, whatever else he is, the acting president. He has taken on a role and a title that he was not born into like a hereditary monarch. No actor is more like King Lear than any other, he is just able to give a more or less convincing performance. And, by the same token, no president is more or less like the president; we can compare his performance only with the performance of other presidents and with the wished-for president in our minds (even if we don't always want to think of presidents as performers, as in show business). It is an obvious point, but one worth bearing in mind. Acting madness, whatever else it means, means acting according to certain conventions; even if there is an important sense in which madness is, by definition, unconventional behaviour. Or that the people we call mad are, of necessity – just like some of the people we value most – people who are unable or unwilling to live conventional lives; to live, that is, by the conventions of their given cultures. There is not an original or ur-King Lear, or President of the United States, or mad person. After five hundred years of professionalized classification and treatment of the so-called mad, at least in the West, there is now a culture of the mad; recognized genres or forms of what began to be called, in Shakespeare's lifetime, 'insanity' (the *OED* has the first use of 'insanity' as 1590, with the first use of 'insanitary' in 1874, one use tellingly leading to the other). And clearly one of the things that diagnosis does is add parts to the cultural repertoire. It becomes more and more difficult to be 'originally' mad; to avoid having a recognizable condition (and when we use the word 'mad' we don't mean idiosyncratic). It is both comforting and confining – and can, indeed, be life-saving – when people in the know claim to know what we are suffering from. But mad people, as all these plays dramatize, make people jump to conclusions about them (anxiety makes people jump to conclusions); madness tempts people to be more knowing than they are. It certainly makes people work because they have something about someone that has to be dealt with (the mad are trying to make themselves impossible to ignore and impossible not to want to ignore).

It is part of the art of these three plays that to begin with we do not think of the protagonists as what Ralph

Waldo Emerson called 'representative men', or as ordinary people; and by the end we think of them as both. And yet during the plays the heroes get progressively stranger. Acting madness in these plays means acting a character who becomes increasingly opaque to himself. There is not a cure, but a catastrophe. The plays are something other than therapeutic, something less instrumental in their intent. But these plays dramatize the relationship between the hero's need and his sociability, as all dramas do. The difference – which is not entirely a difference between the dramas of the mad and the dramas of the normal – or, shall we say, the dramas of the less mad – is that the mad tend to be defined by the obscurity of their need and the threat their sociability entails. Acting madness means acting this obscurity and this threat.

There is, then, real madness, which may or may not be, as we say, 'treated', and actors acting madness on the stage; and the fact that madness – which is itself a form of contention, a being-at-odds – has always been a contentious issue, with its own history, and set of more or less consensual definitions. And, by the same token, there has always been the ever-present question of whether the mad are, in one sense or another, acting their madness, malingering or dissembling, and what we might mean by saying this (if they are acting, why might they be doing this – to what end? – and how have they learned how to do it? Where have they got their lines from?). Poor Tom's acting of the acting of madness is in stark contrast to Lear's madness. Pretending to be ill may be one of the first – or at least one of the most significant, one of the most formative – performances of childhood; acting as a means to an end. Certainly madness is often deemed to be theatrical in a way that sanity is not (as though one of our tacit definitions of the sane is that they are good at getting their needs known and met). And there are sometimes intimations that the theatricality of madness cuts both ways; that just as there is something theatrical about madness, there is also something mad about theatricality, about people acting out of character, pretending to be people they know they are not, speaking other people's words, letting other people have all the lines and all the best lines. As though theatre and madness are somehow inextricably linked; that madness tests the theatrical illusion, or the limits of theatre, like nothing else (or even that madness exposes something about theatricality, about the impulse behind it, about what it's driving at; as though, say, there is something theatrical about being desiring creatures, that desiring is first and foremost a drama).

But real madness breaks the social bond, and acting madness must not: the mad person's sociability is by definition precarious; the acting of madness, as I say, has to be engaging. Acting madness means holding and keeping people's attention; being mad means always being about to lose it, or living as if it has always already been lost. Or that it can never be recovered. Acting madness is about getting people to be attentive in a different kind of way. Madness transforms the nature of our attention, the quality of our attention, when it doesn't actually destroy our willingness to attend. Theatre has been the precursor of, and the parallel text to – and possibly an antidote for – the medicalization of madness, the invention of what Philip Rieff called 'therapeutic man', and indeed 'the triumph of the therapeutic'. In psychoanalysis – one among many of these transformed forms of attention at once demanded and created by those people disturbed by modern life – the analyst listens to the 'mad' person, or to the madness in the person, sees very little of his life, and speaks; the specified aim, the project of the so-called treatment, is the transformation of suffering through redescription. In the theatre the madness is impersonated, the drama is enacted, and the audience, at least the modern polite audience, listens. The play, of course, is scripted; the psychoanalyst shows the patient how he uses his script to defend himself against his madness. The psychoanalysis, at least by intention, is therapeutic if not actually curative; the theatrical performance does not circumscribe its aims. In one of these social forms the listener is paid, and in the other he pays. What the theatre world and the profession of psychoanalysis both believe is that the mad are worth listening to; indeed, may be among the people who are most worth listening to. Or, to put it slightly differently, the mad parts of ourselves may be the parts (in both senses) worth taking in. But it may be very important that there is somewhere in a culture where people must pay to listen to the mad, rather than the other way round. Somewhere where it is shown that madness – or, rather, madness unmet – is, among many other things, radical self-destructiveness, and that, at the end, there may be someone else that one can return to being. Where it can be borne in mind that madness can be at once a fate and a role; that if, say, it is learned, it might be unlearned. That if it is dumb, repetitive, or terrifying, it can be eloquent, startling and moving. And that radical self-destructiveness can be a form of radical self-knowledge.

When an actor or actress is acting madness, there are two degrees of separation, two vital differences in play for the actor and the audience; two differences that the viability of a play as a play, as an illusion, depends upon. When we see the acting of madness in the theatre, two assumptions are always made, which the plays themselves often question; if either the actors or the audience begin to seriously doubt at least one of these assumptions during the performance it would become a discomfiting if not actually unbearable experience. It is assumed that there is a difference between sanity and madness, and a difference, which the theatrical illusion depends upon, between being mad and acting the part of a mad person. If we began to have the feeling that the people playing, as we say, Lear or the Macbeths were really as mad as they seem to be in their plays, being a member of the audience would become very much more disturbing. Of course there are good reasons why Goneril and Regan, or the Macbeths, are not going to harm us, but what terrorizes us about the mad is their unpredictability; we never quite know whom they will address, what they will want, and how they will want it; we never know who they think we are (as though the sane are predictable, and do know who we are). And so acting madness depends upon the audience being sufficiently but not overwhelmingly convinced, not unthreatened but not so threatened as to take cover; in these plays we give madness an audience – or madness, like a king, gives us an audience – but we don't want to be driven mad (we want the contagion of madness – the intense, persecutory feeling and self-doubt madness evokes in us – contained). Both the actor and the audience have to keep their distance from something, when madness is itself about the keeping and losing of distance.

The madness that is in real life an excessive and paradoxical form of distance regulation – the mad invite and repel our attention often simultaneously – enacted in the theatre has to make the repelling of attention as alluring, as intriguing, as the courting of attention. And so the theatrical representation of madness can't help but make us wonder what kind of audience the really mad create for themselves, along the lines of the psychoanalyst D. W. Winnicott's suggestion that if we want to understand a person and their symptoms we need to see what kind of environment they create for themselves, what sort of world they make (a so-called symptom, for example, might be like a rule other people have to abide by, a love-test or a conversation-stopper). What Winnicott means by the 'environment' a person creates around them is what people call up in other people, what versions of other people they induce or preclude, through their symptoms, through the ways they make a nuisance of themselves. Lear, for example, at the beginning of the play, calls up in his love-test a family of two servile and demonically manipulative daughters and one peculiarly truthful daughter. Whether or not they were like this before, they are like this now. When madness is enacted in the theatre, there is the environment that Lear or the Macbeths or Poprishchin create around them – the effects and consequences their madness have, what the people around them turn into – and a different kind of environment called the audience. What the psychoanalyst shares with, or learns from, the contemporary theatre audience is the tacit belief that, when it comes to madness, you speak only after you have heard as much as you can.

But it is worth noticing, when thinking about at least the contemporary theatre audience, that there are distinctions in play – between sanity and madness, between acting and being ourselves – a lot of us have been educated to be particularly suspicious of. And our suspicion, in its turn, makes the modern experience of acting madness, of seeing madness enacted on the stage, very much more disturbing; and the more disturbing something is, the more ingenious are the defences called up to protect ourselves from it (and Macbeth himself tells us how we can all too well inure ourselves to terror: 'I have almost forgot the taste of fears,' he says in Act V, scene 5, and it is a warning to the audience; 'I have supp'd full with horrors; / Direness, familiar to my slaughterous thoughts / Cannot once start me'.) We, or at least some of us, have been persuaded to believe that there are not, alas, two kinds of people, the sane and the mad, but that there is, as we say, a continuum that we are all on; that we are all an uneasy mixture of the two, if there are two such states; or even that we make this reassuring distinction because we know somewhere how blurred the boundaries are; that a lot of so-called sanity is crazy, and that there is a lot of sanity in so-called madness. And indeed that there is some kind of complicity between the nominally sane and the nominally mad. And just as sanity and madness may be secret sharers, there may be no more to a person, as Macbeth famously wonders, than the parts they play (doubts about essentialism have a long history). That is to say, all those people who no longer believe in an essential self – or, indeed, in an essential anything – people who don't need the God-terms, who no longer find words like 'true' or 'authentic' or 'real' any use, are drawn to more performative accounts of the self; they think of the 'self' as a word to cover the repertoire of performances desired by them and demanded of them in a particular culture, at a particular time. This is what Irving Goffman called 'the presentation of self in everyday life' and Stephen Greenblatt calls 'self-fashioning'; a presentation is made, there is a fashioning, the language of artefacts replaces the language of nature. For these people there are not true and false selves but preferred selves; when I say that something is 'not really me,' I'm not saying this is against the grain, as though there is a grain that I am; I'm saying that for a variety of reasons I don't want to be or do whatever it is. I can't be anything I want, but there is more to me than I know. In this view sanity and madness are two of our culturally inherited roles or parts or options; we may not choose them in a way an actor might choose a role, but we may choose them in the way an animal tries to find an environment that works for it, or the way in which someone who bets on horses tries to pick a winner. And there is nothing else we can do but perform ourselves.

There is no alternative to acting, no binary opposite for us to prefer. All the world's a stage and there are no other worlds. We are always and only acting, and the question asked in *Twelfth Night* – 'Are all the people mad?' – has been answered in the affirmative. Madness is part of our potential; whether we are born mad (as some psycho-analysts believe) or driven mad or are genetically predisposed to madness, as many people now seem to believe, madness is part of our make-up, so to speak; but no one is exempt from the possibility of madness, and everyone recognizes something of themselves in the mad, if they can bear to. So it is worth reiterating the philosopher J. L. Austin's question from *Sense and Sensibilia*: 'When you say, "It's real" – what exactly are you saying it isn't?'; and asking, what is someone who is not mad, being?; what is someone who is not acting, doing?

There is a world in which these issues are still alive as questions – are we all actors? Are we all somewhere mad? – and a world in which these things have already been decided, one way or another. Sometimes we are inclined to think one thing, and sometimes the other; our moods, as Emerson remarked, don't believe in each other. And acting madness, needless to say, looks rather different and is a rather different project in each of these worlds; or, rather, from these two quite different perspectives. It is uncontentious to say, I think, that when these two Shakespeare plays and Gogol's original story were written, these issues were in question, were indeed being worked out, among other things, in these writings and performances. And it would be naive to say that many of these questions have now been answered; but there will be people in a contemporary audience who will, to all intents and purposes, believe – that is, be living as if – these issues have been decided, either way. These people, some of us, some of the time, know that whatever else we are, we are also mad; and that we can at least sometimes experience ourselves not as so-called multiple personalities, but as people with several often incompatible versions of ourselves; as people who have some choice as to how they act, and who can easily think of themselves as wanting to improve their performances. What begins as pathology can soon become the norm; the shock of the new and the pathologizing of the new can be inextricable. Now everyone's mad, and everyone's playing roles; or, as some of the professions will tell us, some people are mad in the sense that some people have cancer, and people who act in real life are 'as-if personalities', estranged from their true selves, people who have overadapted to harmful environments at the cost of their own desire. Is being able to act, and particularly to act well, a symptom of estrangement, or a sign of virtuosity and resilience?

This is, of course, partly a caricature, and partly not. And it is very difficult to talk about madness now because capitalist medicine depends on differential diagnoses, that is, the creation of drug markets; and because diagnosis in the so-called mental health professions is, for various reasons, not by any means all nefarious, more sophisticated, in both senses, than ever before. Anyone who has worked in these professions for more than ten minutes knows how quickly fashions and diagnoses change; when I started working as a child psychotherapist there were several years during which many children were deemed to be suffering from ADD (attention deficit disorder) and were treated accordingly, sometimes with drugs, but this fad passed; now it seems that everyone is bipolar. So-called mental health, that is to say, is normative; and the norms are created by consensus (and the consensus can be created, as it is now, by both science and the market, by both telling us the truth about reality, and that mental illness is real in the same way that physical illness is). If Lear or the Macbeths or Poprishchin were living with us now, there would be professionals who would know what was wrong with them, treat them accordingly, and we wouldn't have needed all this drama, all this talk. Less said soonest mended. To be drugged is not always to have been heard; when it comes to madness the theatre has always been the best antidote to the drug-culture. The theatre has always been the real antipsychiatry movement.

But there is one simple distinction that can usefully be made, one description that has the considerable virtue of being of a piece with ordinary non-specialist language, and which reveals how interesting and enigmatic the acting of madness can be, both for the actors and the audience; and this is that we call people mad when they are unintelligible and / or when they behave in ways that are excessively disturbing. The mad are people we can't understand and who do things that are too unacceptable; and so they are people we may be, or feel ourselves to be, endangered by. They expose what an enormous cultural investment we have in understanding people; madness, we could almost say, is what makes us idealize understanding each other, and makes us want to believe that we do. 'Madness,' the British analyst John Rickman once remarked, 'is when you can't find anyone who can stand you' (by the end of these plays the heroes cannot find anyone, including themselves, who can stand them; but we can more than stand them, and the plays they are in; indeed, we can't, as yet, forget them). In terms of theatre, what this means is that the actor acting madness – and this is done partly by the contained frame of the stage itself – has to make the madness, as I say, sufficiently compelling; which in itself conveys the sense that there is something compelling about madness. The mad person – like Lear, like Macbeth, like the hero of *Diary of a Madman*, as their dramas unfold – has difficulty finding anyone who can stand them; this is their quest. But the person acting the mad character has to be utterly alluring; what we might be unable to stand we must also find irresistibly compelling.

The dramatizing and the acting of madness has to be sufficiently intelligible and sufficiently unthreatening to engage the audience, so they can avoid doing what they are often inclined to do in so-called real life, which is, in one way or another, to turn away; to identify with, or to prefer, the forces of containment and punishment – the police and the doctors – rather than the mad person himself. The theatrical representation of madness offers us the opportunity of finding out what the opposite or the alternative is to turning a blind eye; it offers us the opportunity to allow ourselves to identify with the mad – indeed, in a certain sense, to celebrate the mad. The theatrical representation of madness opposes the scapegoating of the mad, and shows how it works. It finds a way of including madness in our culture, without the exclusive and excluding project of treating it. Acting madness means being mad in a way that doesn't make you beyond the pale; that doesn't leave the mad only in the hands of the experts ('I will show you fear in a handful of specialists,' John Ashbery writes in *Flow Chart*). So the actor acting madness is faced with the same dilemma of the mad person himself: how can I say what I have to say, in the way I can say it, without being silenced by the determined deafness and the terror of others? To act the thing that everyone is most frightened of – to be able to do that, to act madness almost as powerfully as the thing itself – changes our sense of what the thing itself is. And we are told this in Act IV, scene 1 of *King Lear* when Edgar says, 'the worst is not / So long as we can say "This is the worst".' If it can be acted, what must it be like not to be acting it? Or not to be able to say 'this is the worst'? What is it about madness that makes us want to dramatize it at all? If at least some of the mad are mad because no one has been able or willing to take in what they say, or see who they are, then anything that makes it possible to listen and to see can only be a good thing (or the sense in which it may or may not be a good thing can be considered), as well as an uncanny repetition of the real thing. In essence: how do I say the unacceptable thing without becoming unacceptable myself?

Yet because madness is so ultimately disturbing to us, it tends to polarize our responses: either we discipline and punish the mad or we idealize them as oracles; or we aestheticize them, staging them as heroes, so that as an audience (or as readers) we are exhilarated and moved by things we would never want to undergo. And this too the theatre is complicit with; we might argue about who the heroes of *Macbeth* and *Lear* and *Diary of a Madman* are, but we will all too easily call the mad protagonists the heroes of these plays (and we may wonder now, what, if anything, is heroic about madness? What kind of heroes can the mad be now, in the cultures we live in, when we are encouraged to think of them as patients, as ill or genetically disabled, as losers and scroungers, as people who have nothing to contribute?). It is clearly another version of the perennial modern question: how can we re-present the unacceptable to ensure that it gets a hearing? And, of course, why do we want to do this? Why do we want to aspire to inclusiveness? And what are the alternatives? And how can we ensure that the hearing the mad are given is not merely a glamorization, a mockery or a covert dismissal?

The Fool in *Lear* can make us wonder whether the mad are oracular or banal or a mockery of both; the Fool at least performs the asking of such questions in a way that is at once both riveting and baffling. What we should do with the mad is bound up with the question of what we think the mad are doing. It was the anti-psychiatry movement in the 1960s that in its genuinely enlightening eagerness not to dismiss the mad was sometimes, ironically, inclined to the different heartless-ness of overvaluing their experience ('Madness,' David Cooper, one of R. D. Laing's collaborators, wrote in his Introduction to Michel Foucault's *Madness and Civilization*, 'has in our age become some sort of lost truth'; Laing, always more sympathetic and circumspect than Cooper, wrote that 'sometimes . . . transcendental experiences . . . break through in psychosis'). Lionel

Trilling, after quoting Laing and Cooper in his engaging critique of the antipsychiatry movement in *Sincerity and Authenticity*, says the sensible and true thing that would have to be considered in any contemporary account of acting madness:

But who that has spoken, or tried to speak, with a psychotic friend will consent to betray the masked pain of his bewilderment and solitude by making it the paradigm of liberation from the imprisoning falsehoods of an alienated social reality? Who that finds intelligible the sentences which describe madness (to use that word that cant prefers) in terms of transcendence and charisma will fail to penetrate to the great refusal of human connection that they express, the appalling belief that human existence is made authentic by the possession of a power, or the persuasion of its possession, which is not to be qualified or restricted by the co-ordinate existence of any fellow man?

Yet the doctrine that madness is health, that madness is liberation and authenticity, receives a happy welcome from a consequential part of the educated public. And when we have given due weight to the likelihood that those who respond positively to the doctrine don't have it in mind to go mad, let alone insane – it is characteristic of the intellectual life of our culture that it fosters a form of assent which does not involve actual credence – we must yet take it to be significant of our circumstance that many among us find it gratifying to entertain the thought that alienation is to be overcome only by the completeness of alienation, and that alienation completed is not a deprivation or deficiency but a potency.

This might seem a long way from *Lear*, *Macbeth* and *Diary of a Madman*; and Trilling gave this lecture more than forty years ago, in the spring of 1970, so his characterization of what he calls, in a dated phrase, 'the intellectual life of our culture' is itself dated. And yet in his scepticism about privileging the mad, or madness itself, he says something inadvertently important about acting madness – about madness in the theatre. If the antipsychiatrists are sometimes guilty, like the mad, of a 'great refusal of human connection', of valuing powers 'not to be qualified or restricted by the co-ordinate existence of any fellow man', then the theatrical representation of madness would seem to be the opposite. If madness, whatever else it is, is a breakdown in sociability, is a homelessness – madness is when you can't find anyone who can stand you – then the theatre re-presents, re-circulates, the experiences of the mad among their fellow men and women. As I say, we can more than stand the characters in these plays, and the plays themselves. They entertain us by letting us entertain experiences that we would rather not bear or even think about at all. And certainly none of these three plays entertains the thought 'that alienation is to be overcome only by the completeness of alienation'.

If madness is a form of estrangement, acting madness familiarizes us with the direst forms estrangement can take. If, as Winnicott remarked, 'madness is the need to be believed', in acting madness, it is the performance that needs to be believed; and if it is, when it works, believing in the performance frees us to disbelieve – or to escape the whole world of believing and disbelieving – to wonder about the mad person's need to be believed; especially by himself.

What the mad person most needs to be believed is that he has the solution; but he doesn't know what the problem is that he has the solution to. As each of these plays shows, the solution comes before the problem; the solution is the form the problem takes. Each of these plays begins, as I mentioned earlier, with the hero's solution – Lear's solution is a love-test, Macbeth's a usurpation, Poprishchin's to find out what the dogs have to say – and what unfolds, what comes to light through the drama of the play, through the acting of the madness, is what the problem was. First the solution, then the problem. So each of the plays begins in an atmosphere of plausibility, or at least of possibility; a solution quickly offers itself. And then it is the plausibility, the possibility, that unravels. These plays agree with Freud that we are at our craziest when we are most plausible to ourselves.

Acting madness, then, means acting out the determined not-knowing of something that the hero can't help but know. He is, in the words of the song, the first to know and the last to find out.

'What is most difficult to resolve and cure,' the psychoanalyst Masud Khan wrote in *The Privacy of the Self*, 'is the patient's practice of self-cure. To cure a cure is the paradox that faces us . . .' Symptoms are always a form of self-cure; you first hear about your problem from your proposed solutions to it. The alcoholic is suffering from whatever conflict alcohol was initially a solution to, and then the solution becomes the problem. The real question is not, how can someone stop drinking, but rather what was the alcohol a self-cure for in the first place? So in thinking about these plays, and particularly about the acting of madness, we need to think of madness as a form of self-cure; a self-cure so drastic that the original problem or illness or predicament – it is difficult to know what the right word is – is utterly lost track of. The problem is cast into oblivion by the solution. So we need to be wary of solutions that make the problem, to all intents and purposes, disappear: neither Shakespeare nor Gogol (nor David Holman) do this; they keep the problem alive in the solution. As does the actor acting the madness. Where once there were terrible self-doubts, there are now tremendous states of conviction; where once there might have been paralysis, there is now immeasurable possibility; where once there was, however unconsciously, a tortured soul, now there is a pragmatist, a man who knows what is to be done, and that something can be done. And then the catastrophe gradually seeps back in. It is the attempt to enforce a solution that reveals the problem. We see each of the protagonists pushing their plans forward; and each of the heroes, it is worth noting, claims, at least at the outset, to know exactly what he wants. Tragic heroes are consistent in their wanting; and make us wonder, by the same token, about what kinds of consistent wanting we call mad, or how insistent wanting has to be before we call it mad. When I want to be continually treated as though I am the King of Spain – and each of the heroes of these plays wants to be treated as a king – there is something wrong with me only because I am not the King of Spain; is there something wrong with the real King of Spain – wrong, that is, for him – in always wanting this? The person acting these protagonists is involved in the ironizing of states of conviction; certain kinds of demand, made in certain ways, make us think someone is acting mad. The person playing the mad person has to be at once convincingly convinced – believe in his script – but enacting their conviction in a way that renders it unconvincing to the audience.

The acting of madness involves a knowing scepticism about self-certainty, as though madness was a kind of bravado (like acting itself); an invitation for someone to come along and say 'get over yourself', or 'that is not it at all'. The mad hero delegates his self-doubting to the audience. The audience is overhearing something; they are overhearing someone tormenting himself by tormenting others. The mad can't speak to themselves because they can't speak to others. So when the mad are offered another audience – the audience outside the drama – it is like their being offered another kind of hope. There is the closed possibility of the drama enacted on stage, something with a beginning, a middle and an end; and there is the open possibility – the unscripted consequences – of the witnessed drama felt and thought about by each member of the audience.

I think it is worth considering that the audience for tragedy perhaps, and certainly for the performance of madness, has a different role, is put in a different position than the audience for other predicaments. The by now rather academic question, why does tragedy give pleasure? can be rephrased in this context by the, in some ways more daunting question: why (or how) does madness – or, rather, the acting of madness – give pleasure? And particularly, perhaps, why does exceptional acting of madness give exceptional pleasure; and, more exactly, what kind of pleasure is this? Tragedies both on and off the stage are famously gripping; most forms of off-stage madness, as Trilling makes clear, are not. Indeed the privileging of madness, as a cultural moment, was notably short-lived (as was the sometimes useful sense of the mad as tragic heroes and heroines). There has been the all-too-successful medicalization of madness, the differential diagnosis of madness, and the institutionalization of madness; and there was, as I have said, for what seems in retrospect to those who lived through it, merely a moment – inspired most notably by the works of Laing, Cooper, Szasz and Foucault with their talismanic titles – *The Divided Self, The Death of the Family, The Myth of Mental Illness* and *History of Madness* – in which there was an attempt both to redescribe madness as a form of culturally exempted intelligence and to see what the so-called sane were using the mad to do for them (how the culture delegates its dirty work to the so-called mad, and then calls them mad). In both these approaches, at their most extreme, the mad have been both negatively and positively scapegoated; idealized as poets, treated and / or punished as terrifying saboteurs of the social world; seen as people to be listened to or as people to be shut up. Indeed, one of the most striking things about the mad is how difficult they are to be kind to; or how they force us to reconsider what it might be to be kind. The play, and the theatre, in which madness is spoken and enacted is a transitional space in which the mad are incarcerated (or held); in which they can be both idealized and punished, and neither, at the same time; in which they can, as they do in each of these plays, talk at length in their own way, be listened to and, if need be, killed, and yet not really die. And in which the audience can more or less engage with their experience without, in all likelihood, being too much at risk. And the audience in the theatre – unlike the mad hero and his associates; and, indeed, unlike an analyst – are relieved of the burden of looking for solutions, of problem-solving. The audience has to do nothing but attend. And bear with what happens.

And, of course, seeing these plays – we don't speak of hearing plays – is dramatically unlike what Trilling called speaking or trying to speak 'with a psychotic friend'. If all the mad were like the Macbeths or Lear, or Propishchin in David Holman's remarkable play, visiting mental hospitals, or indeed psychotic friends, would be a rather different, sometimes more riveting, experience. If the mad could speak like this, we might think, they would be worth listening to (it may, perhaps, be worth remarking that Shakespeare's demand on the listener is as excessive in its way as the demand of Trilling's psychotic friend; and in both cases it is amazing what you can sometimes hear when you listen). The paradoxical problem of the actors playing these 'mad' roles is that they have, at least potentially, an avid audience, hungry for their words and the drama involved. It is like the telling of a joke. If I tell the audience what I think of as a great joke and no one laughs, I might think, with inner superiority, that it was pearls before swine; but if the audience don't laugh, it not only ceases to be a good joke to anyone other than me, it, in one sense, ceases to be a joke at all. I might just think that it may not be as good a joke as I thought, that my sense of humour was a bit odd. But I may think, logically, that if no one laughs, it is not a joke; and that I clearly no longer know what a joke is. Me and my joke begin to feel insubstantial, not the real thing. I thought I was sociable, that I, as they say, shared a sense of humour, but I have discovered in telling this unamusing joke that I am an isolate; just as you can't have a completely private language, so you can't have an entirely private sense of humour. That is to say, the person acting madness is always having to deal with the question, can a joke be better than its audience? Which translates as, are the mad person's words really words if no one gets them? And if they are not words, what are they? Acting madness means speaking your lines as though they make sense and as though they don't; as though they have a sense, but no one has yet quite got it. In each of these plays it is the progressive not-getting of the mad character's words that drives him mad, that destroys him. And getting it, in this context, as with a joke, doesn't necessarily mean understanding it, but being able to be engaged by it. As Freud says, we rarely understand what it is about a joke that amuses us. So too we rarely really know what it is about the mad person that disturbs us. But we do seem to know when the acting of madness works for us. And it is the connection between these two things that is worth wondering about.

Acknowledgements

The initial sketch for this book was in an essay entitled 'On Getting Away with It', which was published in *On Balance*; the chapter with the same title in this book is a quite different essay, but with overlapping preoccupations. Different versions of 'On Satisfaction' and the first part of 'On Getting Out of It' were published in *Raritan* and *Threepenny Review* respectively; a different version of 'Acting Madness' was also published in *Threepenny Review*, and I am grateful, as ever, to the editors of these journals. Several of the chapters of this book were first given as lectures at the University of York; I have benefited greatly from the responses of colleagues and students. I have been extremely fortunate to be a member of Geoffrey Weaver's reading group; many things in this book have been informed by our discussions. Hugh Haughton has, as ever, been somehow essential in the writing of this, and indeed of all my other books. Judith Clark has made virtually everything possible.

Permissions Acknowledgements

Grateful acknowledgement is made for permission to reprint the following material:

- Lines from *Charisma*, by Philip Rieff, with thanks to Alfred A. Knopf, a division of Random House, Inc. (US).
- Extract from *History and Imagination*, by Hugh Trevor-Roper, reprinted by permission of Peters, Fraser and Dunlop (www.petersfraseranddunlop.com) on behalf of the Estate of Hugh Trevor-Roper.
- #21 from 'Vectors 2.3: 50 Aphorisms and Ten-Second Essays', by James Richardson, from *By the Numbers: Poems and Aphorisms*. Copyright © 2010 by James Richardson. Reprinted with the permission of The Permissions Company, Inc., on behalf of Copper Canyon Press, www.coppercanyonpress.org.
- Lines from 'Reply to Papini', by Wallace Stevens, from *Collected Poems*, reproduced by permission of Pollinger Limited; Alfred A. Knopf, a division of Random House, Inc. (US); and Faber and Faber Ltd.
- 'This Be the Verse', by Philip Larkin, from *High Windows*, reprinted by kind permission of Faber and Faber Ltd. and The Society of Authors as the Literary Representative of the Estate of Philip Larkin.
- Lines from 'Hearsay', by John Burnside, from *Black Cat Bone*, reproduced by kind permission of Rogers, Coleridge and White Ltd., on behalf of Jonathan Cape, The Random House Group.
- Permission for the use of the quotation from *Collected Poems*, by Marianne Moore, 1967, is granted by the Literary Estate of Marianne C. Moore, David M. Moore, Esq., Administrator. All rights reserved.

A Note About the Author

Adam Phillips is a psychoanalyst and a visiting professor in the English department at the University of York. He is the author of many books, including *On Kissing, Tickling, and Being Bored*; *Going Sane*; *Side Effects*; and *On Balance*. He is also the co-author, with the historian Barbara Taylor, of *On Kindness*; with the critic Leo Bersani, of *Intimacies*; and with the exhibition-maker Judith Clark, of *The Concise Dictionary of Dress*.